# WOMEN PASTORS, WHY NOT?

BIBLE ILLUMINATIONS

*Louis R. Torres*

## ABOUT THE BOOK

This book springs out of the many years of experience laboring to satisfy the clamoring cry for effective training on the part of men and women that have been marginalized or seriously limited by finance, formal education, race, gender, and social norms. Many ladies have found themselves caught behind these same fences. To those on the 'outside' wistfully looking to be part of the groundswell of those 'preparing the way of the Lord', I dedicate this book - with special attention to the Mothers of Israel ("the hand that rocks the cradle, rules the world").

## ABOUT THE AUTHOR

Pastor Torres' more than forty-five years of service-oriented ministry, both outside and inside the confines of the official church organization, gives him a very unique view of the Family of God. Being raised in the Ghettos of New York City, he learned at a very young age that you do not mess with someone's mother, especially your own. Sometimes, every 'brother' did not feel the same way and there would be internal and bitter fights; but in the end it was all for the 'mother'. As he translates this life lesson into the spiritual realm, he realizes that what is truly for the 'mother' is also truly for the wellbeing of the 'brothers'. His careful analysis and clear explanations will cause you to think, reflect, and contemplate your intentions and positions in reference to 'the family of God'.

# TABLE OF CONTENTS

# FORWARD

Through 40 years of ministry I have witnessed many attempts to introduce a variety of teachings called "new light." All of those movements have since faded into the pitch darkness of Egypt. After all, that is where many false teachings had their beginnings. Well do I remember the consternation and anxiety each group brought. There were the Brinsmeadites, who were followers of Robert Daniel Brinsmead in the 1960s; the Shepherd's Rod; Davidians; proponents of righteousness by faith; the Fordites; etc. Each purported to have new light.

Usually most of these movements began with good people trying to become ever so careful with what they believed. When opposition erupted against their new light, those whom they once considered brothers and sisters they regarded as apostates or enemies of their faith. The years reveal a landscape strewn with the spiritual wreckage of well-meaning people meandering somewhere between unbelief, skepticism, and atheism, or just wounded, and left bitter or callous, thinking that their newfound light outshines the doctrines and teachings they once knew and loved.

Once again the church is rocking and reeling - not from the beat of "Rock Around the Clock," but from well-meaning people anxious to champion a new cause: women's ordination into the gospel ministry.

In my old gang-member days it was considered cowardly to avoid a fight when your buddies were in the throes of a battle. The cause to defend was nothing more than ignorance, racism, or an area they declared to be their turf. Nevertheless, all the members would be committed to give their lives if need be. None of my gang members ever needed to.

Honestly, deep inside I detested having to be dragged in. But there are instances when one feels as though they are experiencing déjà vu. Now I find myself being dragged into another battle. The cause? God's church and His Word! When I was baptized, I vowed to be true and loyal to Christ and His church. If fighting for a worthless cause was considered courageous, certainly getting into the ring for the church is supremely noble.

Frankly, it is difficult to remain silent and watch while the enemy is trying his best to divide and destroy it. Therefore, I am compelled to add my voice to stop the fray. I prayerfully hope what follows will contribute to clear the issue without castigating or being judgmental against anyone.

I am reminded of a statement that jolted me after being guilty of sheepishly hiding my prayer in a restaurant. I had invited a girl-friend to lunch to let her know that I had become a Christian and therefore needed to break off the relationship because the convictions to make matters right were pressing on me. Here I was, a brand new Christian. The restaurant was on 42nd Street in Manhattan, New York City. It was crowded to the hilt. And knowing that in those days it was considered strange to be religious, the pressure was even more intense to avoid being noticed.

When the food came, I felt uncomfortable with the surroundings. The thought came that I should say grace. But I couldn't muster up the courage to just bow my head in the presence of my girlfriend and the multitude around me. I therefore attempted to hide what I was doing. Hoping to avoid the perceived embarrassment I would experience from the stares of the onlooking crowd, I simply pretended that I needed to tie my shoe and, while ducking underneath the table, said grace. After I left the restaurant and her presence, a little voice said to my conscience, "Whosoever therefore shall be ashamed of me and of my words in this adulterous and sinful generation; of him also shall the Son of man be ashamed, when he cometh in the glory of his Father with the holy angels" (Mark 8:38). My, did I feel conscience-stricken!

Later on I found the following statement. "The Lord abhors indifference and disloyalty in a time of crisis in His work. The whole universe is watching with inexpressible interest the closing scenes of the great controversy between good and evil. The people of God are nearing the borders of the eternal world; what can be of more importance to them than that they be loyal to the God of heaven? All through the ages, God has had moral heroes, and He has them now - those who, like Joseph and Elijah and Daniel, are not ashamed to acknowledge themselves His peculiar people. His special blessing accompanies the labors of men of action, men who will not be swerved from the straight line of duty, but who with divine energy will inquire, 'Who is on the Lord's side?' (Exodus 32:26), men who will not stop merely with the inquiry, but who will demand that those who choose to identify themselves with the people of God shall step forward and reveal unmistakably their allegiance to the King of kings and Lord of lords. Such men make their wills and plans subordinate to the law of God. For love of Him they count not their lives dear unto themselves. Their work is to catch the light from the Word and let it shine forth to the world in clear, steady rays. Fidelity to God is their motto."[1]

## ILLUSTRIOUS WOMEN IN THE OLD TESTAMENT

In Holy Writ there is recorded a number of women and their role in history. Paul reminds us of the intent of their indelible registration. "Now all these things happened unto them for ensamples: and they are written for our admonition, upon whom the ends of the world are come" (1 Corinthians 10:11). Peter, also describing the example of the women of the Old Testament, wrote, "For after this manner in the old time the holy women also, who trusted in God, adorned themselves, being in subjection unto their own husbands: Even as Sara obeyed Abraham, calling him lord: whose daughters ye are, as long as ye do well, and are not afraid with any amazement" (1 Peter 3:5, 6). God has included the experiences of women and men as lessons for all peoples. We are admonished to learn from their examples, mistakes, deeds, faithfulness, unfaithfulness, words, and yes, silence.

---

1 *ELLEN G. WHITE, PROPHETS AND KINGS, P. 148*

The first woman, Eve, was the "mother of all living" (Genesis 3:20). Lofty and elevated was to be her position. What other woman in the annals of history could share the prestigious title of being the mother of the human race! From the start God honored women with the endearing, noble, and sacred designation of being called mother. Think of it!

What is to be learned from her experience? Some may wonder why Eve left Adam's side. Good question! The biblical narratives, while they do not explicitly state, the reason Eve left Adam's side and fell, suggest that in his absence she toyed with the aspiration of superiority when Satan tempted her. The insightful apostle Paul, by inspiration, sheds light into the motivation contributing to her fall. He wrote, "But I suffer not a woman to teach, nor to usurp authority over the man. . . . And Adam was not deceived, but the woman being deceived was in the transgression. Notwithstanding she shall be saved in childbearing, if they continue in faith and charity and holiness with sobriety" (1 Timothy 2:12-15).

Inspiration states, "Satan found Eve willing to listen to his temptations, and [he] read a disposition to distrust the word of God. . . ."[2] The Tempter claimed, "Ye shall be as gods knowing good and evil" (Genesis 3:5). "That knowledge was obtained, but what a knowledge it was! The curse of sin was the knowledge they gained. Eve coveted the thing God had forbidden. She revealed a distrust of God and His goodness, and a desire to be independent and do as she thought best. Eve offered the fruit to Adam and became his tempter. She would be a god. She would be a law unto herself. She would acknowledge no restraint. But that apparently smallest of sins constituted her a transgressor of the law of God"[3]

"Eve had been perfectly happy by her husband's side in her Eden home; but, like restless modern Eves, she was flattered with the hope of entering a higher sphere than that which God had assigned her. In attempting to rise above her original position, she fell far below it. A similar result will be reached by all who are unwilling

---

2 *ELLEN G.WHITE, CHRIST TRIUMPHANT, P. 22.*

3 *IBID.*

to take up cheerfully their life duties in accordance with God's plan. In their efforts to reach positions for which He has not fitted them, many are leaving vacant the place where they might be a blessing. In their desire for a higher sphere, many have sacrificed true womanly dignity and nobility of character, and have left undone the very work that Heaven appointed them."[4]

She nonetheless regains her bearings as she gives evidence to where her confidence should have been placed. Recognizing that her hope and deliverance would come from the man-child, she is recorded as stating: "For God, said she, hath appointed me another seed instead of Abel, whom Cain slew. And to Seth, to him also there was born a son; and he called his name Enos: then began men to call upon the name of the Lord" (Genesis 4:25, 26). Using the term seed, she alludes to the promise given her by God Himself when He said,
"And I will put enmity between thee and the woman, and between thy seed and her seed; it shall bruise thy head, and thou shalt bruise his heel. Unto the woman he said, I will greatly multiply thy sorrow and thy conception; in sorrow thou shalt bring forth children; and thy desire shall be to thy husband, and he shall rule over thee" (Genesis 3:15, 16).

Hence, this is the reason for the apparently chauvinistic biblical slant. It was imperative that God's offer of a Savior to humanity through the man-child would be kept track of. No wonder that several genealogical lists are found in the Scriptures. In the book of Luke there is a long list tracing the seed all the way from Christ to being "the son of Adam, which was the son of God" (Luke 3:38; see verses 23-38 for the entire list). This truth would hold in check any notion, practice, or idea that the world's savior is Mary or any other woman. Salvation for humanity must come by a man-child born of a woman.

There are other notable women, such as Sarah, Abraham's wife, who at the age of 90 miraculously gave birth to Isaac. "And God said unto Abraham, As for Sarai thy wife, thou shalt not call her name Sarai, but Sarah shall her name be. And I will bless her, and give

---

4 *ELLEN G.WHITE, PATRIARCHS AND PROPHETS, P. 59.*

thee a son also of her: yea, I will bless her, and she shall be a mother of nations; kings of people shall be of her" (Genesis 17:15, 16). She is considered to be a woman of faith and is registered in the biblical chapter considered by many as the "Hall of Faith" chapter. "Through faith also Sara herself received strength to conceive seed, and was delivered of a child when she was past age, because she judged him faithful who had promised" (Hebrews 11:11). Though she had been told that she would be the "mother of nations; kings of people shall be of her" (Genesis 17:16), she held in check the temptation that came to Eve. The apostle Peter writes, "Even as Sara obeyed Abraham, calling him lord: whose daughters ye are, as long as ye do well" (1 Peter 3:6).

Knowing that her son, Isaac, was to become the heir of promise; and knowing her place, she refused to allow herself and her son to be sidestepped by her rival slave. By demanding Abraham to send Hagar away, she proved that a wife could exercise her rights. And as difficult as it was for Abraham to meet Sarah's insistence, his yielding to her wishes demonstrates that he respected her place in the family. It was a hard lesson for Hagar to learn, but nonetheless, it was an essential decision for Sarah to make. It was a bitter experience also for Sarah. The tuition paid was high for that lesson. Never again did she run ahead of God.

"The birth of Isaac, bringing, after a lifelong waiting, the fulfillment of their dearest hopes, filled the tents of Abraham and Sarah with gladness. But to Hagar this event was the overthrow of her fondly cherished ambitions. Ishmael, now a youth, had been regarded by all in the encampment as the heir of Abraham's wealth and the inheritor of the blessings promised to his descendants. Now he was suddenly set aside; and in their disappointment, mother and son hated the child of Sarah. The general rejoicing increased their jealousy, until Ishmael dared openly to mock the heir of God's promise. Sarah saw in Ishmael's turbulent disposition a perpetual source of discord, and she appealed to Abraham, urging that Hagar and Ishmael be sent away from the encampment."[5] Sarah's haste to accomplish God's will in

---

5 *ELLEN G. WHITE, CHRIST TRIUMPHANT, P. 82.*

her own way set in motion a strife that is still smoldering today. A lesson of what not to do has been left for all future generations.

Yet, another lesson comes from Hagar's side. Perhaps the strife between the two groups of people (Jews and Arabs) would not have existed if Hagar had taken a different posture concerning the position that did not belong to her or her son. At least as far as women are concerned, this is the first recorded struggle over who would have the supremacy, and the terrible outcome of that strife. Her feelings of entitlement led her to hate the child of Sarah. "Flattered with the honor of her new position as Abraham's wife, and hoping to be the mother of the great nation to descend from him, Hagar became proud and boastful, and treated her mistress with contempt."[6] One cannot help wondering whether the affairs of things would have been different in that family if she had not taken the attitude of entitlement. It is that same spirit that still incites not only the present struggle between Abraham's descendants, but also the great controversy between Satan and God.

Rachel and Leah, who were sisters, were first cousins to Jacob and nieces to his mother, Rebekah, who was the sister of Laban, their father. Though there was sister sibling rivalry, which in turn contributed to Jacob's children's sibling rivalry, they are attributed as being the mothers of Israel. Concerning Ruth the Moabite, the leaders told Boaz, "The Lord make the woman that is come into thine house like Rachel and like Leah, which two did build the house of Israel" (Ruth 4:11). These women grew up in dysfunctional situations. Nevertheless, they ultimately made decisions that altered their future, making them examples of victorious women worthy of emulation, not of their former state, but of their final victory.

Had it not been for a mother's love that was mightier than Pharaoh's decree, braving whatever consequences to herself, Jochebed would not have saved Moses. Her steadfastness in training her son while acting as his nanny contributed to Moses' later awareness of his roots, and decision in casting his lot with God's people (see

---

6 *ELLEN G.WHITE, PATRIARCHS AND PROPHETS, P. 145.*

Hebrews 11:23, 24). What an impact this women had—not only on her son, but also on the world. Well says the poem by William Ross Wallace: "The Hand That Rocks the Cradle Is the Hand That Rules the World."

This story would not be complete without the two other children raised by her: Aaron, and Miriam. Since we are writing about women, let us focus on Miriam. She was obviously Moses' older sister, for it was she who followed the baby-laden basket through the thickets of the bulrushes. Her "on-the-spot" precociousness, at the opportune moment with Pharaoh's princess daughter, gave evidence of the importance of seizing the moment when it arrives. She became a prophet and also a leader among the women (see Exodus 15:20, 21). In that role, she was instrumental in leading the women to acknowledge and praise God for His doings - a noteworthy example, to say the least.

But another lesson to learn from her is to allow the younger brother grow up. Just because she apparently helped her mother with Moses' early childhood did not mean that she could lord it over her baby brother. Nor should a near kinswoman presume to lightly regard a relative's authority or assume equality, especially when God was the one who placed Moses in that position of authority. Later in the book we will cover the details of that sibling rivalry.

Let's consider another great woman. Her name was Deborah. She happened to be a "prophetess" (Judges 4:4). She declares, "Until that I Deborah arose, that I arose a mother in Israel" (Judges 5:7). She was both a judge and a prophetess: a recognized woman in Israel. Yet, she herself maintains her position among the people as a mother, never referring to herself as an elder. She was a women recognized by her peers as a women leader - a mother is considered the female leader of a home. Being considered a mother in Israel made her a counselor, but Barak was the recognized leader. In fact, in the list of the judges who were the recognized leaders in the book of Hebrews, it mentions "Gedeon, and of Barak, and of Samson, and of Jephthae" (Hebrews 11:32). Never was Deborah considered the leader, priest, or king of Israel. Her own mouth testified to her position - she was a mother of Israel.

This standing is obviously recognized as a status for women in Israel who have attained a high stature among the people. When Joab, the general of King David's army, sought for Sheba, a man who had lifted himself up in revolt against David, he "came and besieged him in Abel of Bethmaachah, and they cast up a bank against the city, and it stood in the trench: and all the people that were with Joab battered the wall, to throw it down" (2 Samuel 20:15). Then a "wise woman out of the city" (verse 16) called out to Joab seeking a dialog. When he responded to her call, she asked: "I am one of them that are peaceable and faithful in Israel: thou seekest to destroy a city and a mother in Israel: why wilt thou swallow up the inheritance of the Lord?" (verse 19).

Then Joab answered and said: "Far be it, far be it from me, that I should swallow up or destroy. The matter is not so: but a man of mount Ephraim, Sheba the son of Bichri by name, hath lifted up his hand against the king, even against David: deliver him only, and I will depart from the city" (verses 20, 21). The woman was obviously recognized as a woman of stature in her city, for she told Joab that she could meet his demand. "Then the woman went unto all the people in her wisdom" (verse 22). Her stature was sufficient to sway the people to meet the demands. She returned with the man's head and threw it down to Joab. With this, Joab blew the trumpet, and the entire army retreated having met their aim.

This woman is not named; there is nothing more recorded concerning her lineage, title, parentage, or status. Scripture simply mentions her as a "wise woman," and she refers to herself as a "mother in Israel." Once again there is evidence that among God's people there were women recognized for their wisdom, abilities, and leadership capabilities. Yet, they were never considered elders, but rather "mothers in Israel."

Most of the time those who read the Bible come across lists of names. Many skip over these genealogical grouping of names and go on to easier and less boring reading. Doing so is like two men during the great California gold rush who bought a cave and began digging. They dug for days and days and gained nothing more than sore muscles and a lot of rubble and rocks. They finally decided to sell their interest for a few dollars, and move on to hopefully more prosperous territory. The buyers of the cave dug only two more inches, and the mine made them rich.

Such is the case with Matthew 1. There among the list of great biblical characters, are the names of three women. Tamar, the harlot Rahab, and Ruth the Moabite. There is a fourth, but she is referenced to only as "her that had been the wife of Urias" (verse 6). Her name was Bathsheba, the wife of David, and the mother of Solomon. Through these four women God reveals His glorious love and power to change the lot and destiny of those who are lost.

In Genesis chapter 38 we find the story of Tamar. She was a Canaanite whom the backslidden son of Jacob, Judah, took as a wife for his eldest son. She was defrauded three times by this man and his sons. Though not of Hebrew birth, she had Hebrew aspirations. She was entitled to have a child. And then she saw that her father-in-law was not going to honor his word. "Then said Judah to Tamar his daughter in law, Remain a widow at thy father's house, till Shelah my son be grown: for he said, Lest peradventure he die also, as his brethren did. And Tamar went and dwelt in her father's house" (verse 11). Though she complied with his wishes, she saw in time that Judah had no intentions of keeping his word. He would leave her barren. "And in process of time the daughter of Shuah Judah's wife died" (verse 12). Now Judah was a widower. The Bible does not specified how much time passed. However, it must have been long enough for the young man to grow up and take up his responsibility with Tamar.

You may wonder why Tamar is so anxious to have a baby. All faithful Jewish women knew from the promise of Genesis 3:15 that the hope of humanity rested on the promised seed. From the time Adam and Eve fell, women hoped to be the bearer of the promised seed. This fact becomes crystal clear when God indeed makes her one of those bearers. Tamar did not let herself be cheated again. She took off her widow's garments and went and sat by the wayside. Supposing that she was a prostitute, Judah offered to buy her services. She complied and got pregnant. (Read the story in Genesis 38:6-30.)

When Tamar's father-in-law was sent word that his daughter-in-law was pregnant by whoredom, he demanded she be brought to him and be burnt with fire. In the encounter, she showed the bracelet and staff of the one who got her pregnant. At this revelation Judah said, "She hath been more righteous than I; because that I gave her not to Shelah my son. And he knew her again no more" (Genesis 38:26).

Tamar's surroundings and environment were less than conducive to a pious lifestyle. The family she married into was dysfunctional. Judah was a backslidden son of Jacob, knowing better, but choosing instead to carouse with the heathen. Nevertheless, Tamar, with a sterling character outshining that of her father-in-law's, was determined and hopeful for a better life. In the words of Paul: "For when the Gentiles, which have not the law, do by nature the things contained in the law, these, having not the law, are a law unto themselves: Which shew the work of the law written in their hearts, their conscience also bearing witness" (Romans 2:14, 15).

God honored her with two boys. One of the twins was named Pharez. When the Israelites made the Exodus from Egypt and all the families of Jacob are mentioned, the following is recorded: "And the sons of Judah after their families were; of Shelah, the family of the Shelanites: of Pharez, the family of the Pharzites: of Zerah, the family of the Zarhites. And the sons of Pharez were; of Hezron, the family of the Hezronites: of Hamul, the family of the Hamulites. These are the families of Judah according to those that were numbered of them, threescore and sixteen thousand and five hundred" (Numbers 26:20-22).

No question remains. Tamar is integrated into Jacob's family and leaves with Judah and with her sons to Egypt. Concerning her son Pharez, the Bible says, "Now these are the generations of Pharez: Pharez begat Hezron, and Hezron begat Ram, and Ram begat Amminadab, and Amminadab begat Nahshon, and Nahshon begat Salmon, and Salmon begat Boaz, and Boaz begat Obed, and Obed begat Jesse, and Jesse begat David" (Ruth 4:18-22). Her son becomes one of the ancestors of Christ, and she, one his great-grandmothers.

Think of what God is showing through Tamar. Through this young woman He demonstrates that regardless of one's unfortunate circumstances of life, it does not matter where you come from, or what your background might have been. He can take you out of the muck and mire of life, clean you up, and make of you a child of the King.

The story of Rahab, the harlot, found in Joshua 2 to 6 is even more intriguing. She is a victim of her circumstances and is practicing a shameful occupation. Apparently she is a very young girl. As is still the case in some countries today, it was a practice in those days for families to encourage their daughters to practice prostitution to help with the income. In spite of this, she says to the spies, "For the Lord your God, he is God in heaven above, and in earth beneath" (Joshua 2:11). These do not sound like words coming out of the mouth of a prostitute.

Because of her faith and prompt decision, the prostitute becomes the means of not only her physical deliverance, but also the spiritual salvation of her entire family. The record states, "And the young men that were spies went in, and brought out Rahab, and her father, and her mother, and her brethren, and all that she had; and they brought out all her kindred, and left them without the camp of Israel" (Joshua 6:23). She likewise is honored in that great chapter of faith among the great patriarchs. But what is curiously interesting is that God, in order to demonstrate His power to save even from the depth of sin and degradation, never removes Rahab's title—harlot.
How many of us, in making a résumé or CV, place in there the following: "My grandmother was a prostitute"? Yet in Matthew's genealogical list, God inspired him, a detested and hated publican (see Matthew 9:9; 10:3; Luke 18:10, 11) to place the name of this prostitute. He can relate to her. Though an outcast, he himself is honored in being selected to be among the ones to whom Jesus said, "Ye which have followed me, in the regeneration when the Son of man shall sit in the throne of his glory, ye also shall sit upon twelve thrones, judging the

twelve tribes of Israel" (Matthew 19:28).

Think of it: irrespective of the depths into which the sinner may sink, "he is not ashamed to call them brethren" (Hebrew 2:11). "O the depth of the riches both of the wisdom and knowledge of God! how unsearchable are his judgments, and his ways past finding out! For who hath known the mind of the Lord? or who hath been his counsellor? Or who hath first given to him, and it shall be recompensed unto him again? For of him, and through him, and to him, are all things: to whom be glory for ever. Amen" (Romans 11:33-36).

Once again, God demonstrates through Rahab that His love is more powerful than the filth and dreadful conditions of sin. If He can change and save, and then place such a woman in His genealogy, He can do the same for you. This places all of us within the radar of hope.

The third woman in the list is Ruth, a Moabite. Her people descended from an incestuous relationship between Lot and his daughters. The dark record of that incident states, "Thus were both the daughters of Lot with child by their father. And the firstborn bare a son, and called his name Moab: the same is the father of the Moabites unto this day. And the younger, she also bare a son, and called his name Benammi: the same is the father of the children of Ammon unto this day" (Genesis 19:36-38). "Lot's only posterity, the Moabites and Ammonites, were vile, idolatrous tribes, rebels against God and bitter enemies of His people."[7]

Though she was a pagan, there was a nobility of purpose and genuineness in Ruth. Deep inside there must have been a longing for something better. And when she saw it, she latched onto it. To her Jewish mother-in-law, Naomi, she uttered those famous words that have inspired others to leave their ancestral roots, and choose rather to be part of God's people. She said, "For whither thou goest, I will go; and where thou lodgest, I will lodge: thy people shall be my people, and thy God my God: Where thou diest, will I die, and there

---

7 *ELLEN G.WHITE, PATRIARCHS AND PROPHETS, P. 167.*

will I be buried: the Lord do so to me, and more also, if aught but death part thee and me" (Ruth 1:16, 17).

The words spoken by the women to Naomi about Ruth were these: "Blessed be the Lord, which hath not left thee this day without a kinsman, that his name may be famous in Israel. And he shall be unto thee a restorer of thy life, and a nourisher of thine old age: for thy daughter in law, which loveth thee, which is better to thee than seven sons, hath borne him" (Ruth 4:14, 15). Through Ruth there is born a child that ends up being King David's great-grandfather, and in the direct genealogy of the Savior of the world.

These three women, though victims of their environment, dysfunctional relationships, cultivated and inherited sin and practices, and destined to be destroyed (Exodus 23:23), God used to encourage people of all ages. It does not matter where you have come from or what you have done. If you turn to Christ, He will change your lot. And as the apostle Paul wrote: "Wherefore come out from among them, and be ye separate, saith the Lord, and touch not the unclean thing; and I will receive you, And will be a Father unto you, and ye shall be my sons and daughters, saith the Lord Almighty" (2 Corinthians 6:17, 18). None of these women intruded or pushed themselves into their lofty, providential status of being placed in the prestigious line of honor. They sought only to follow the God of heaven and earth, and in turn, God honored them.

The next illustrious woman was the mother of Samuel the prophet. Her name was Hannah. "Samuel was looked upon by his mother not merely as a child but as an offering to God. Therefore she sought to have him trained for God from his earliest infancy. She ministered to his physical needs with much care and prayer, directing his thoughts toward the Lord of hosts from the very earliest age. That she might the more perfectly fulfill her trust, she did not visit Shiloh till after he was weaned. How far reaching is the influence of a mother in Israel! Whether she be an exile and a slave, like Jochebed the mother of Moses, or the persecuted member of a Levite home in Canaan, her moments are priceless. Realizing this, Hannah began to work not only for time but for eternity. It was her responsibility to impress upon a human soul the image of the divine."[8]

Only in eternity will we know the full extent of that mother's influence over the prophet, Samuel, whom she "lent to the Lord" (1 Samuel 1:28). She is mentioned among many illustrious women who, while maintaining their femininity, exercised their influence over the nations through their children.

In the book of Judges there is the mention of two women who played a decisive role in the overthrow of Sisera and his armies, the enemy of Israel. One is the prophetess Deborah, and the other is Jael, the wife of Heber the Kenite (Judges 4:17). Deborah's courage is highlighted as, at the request of the leaders of Israel, she accompanies the armies into the battlefield (verse 10). By the direction of the Lord, Deborah said to Barak, Israel's leader: "I will surely go with thee: notwithstanding the journey that thou takest shall not be for thine honour; for the Lord shall sell Sisera into the hand of a woman. And Deborah arose, and went with Barak to Kedesh" (verse 9).

This woman apparently had gained such a solid reputation of having a living connection with the Lord that the warrior Barak would not go into battle unless she accompanied him. "Barak said unto her, If thou wilt go with me, then I will go: but if thou wilt not go with me, then I will not go" (verse 8). He obviously did not see her as a mere woman, but rather as a godly woman who was God's messenger. No chauvinism on his part. His respect for her was admirable. His confidence in her godly connection: immovable!

Deborah's God-given prophecy ensured the victory He would give through a woman. The story of the fulfillment of that prophecy is recorded in verses 18-21. She judged "Israel during the reign of Jabin, a Canaanite king who was very cruel to the children of Israel. Life in the villages was harsh. The people were plundered and fled to the fortified cities for protection. Then the Lord raised up Deborah, who was like a loving mother to Israel. God sent a message through her to Barak that he should prepare to meet Sisera, Jabin's general, in battle.

---

8 *THE SDA BIBLE COMMENTARY, VOL. 2, P. 456.*

Barak refused to go unless Deborah went with him. She agreed, but warned him that because of his lack of faith in the words of the Lord, the honor of killing Sisera would go to a woman, not to Barak."[9]

Jael's gentleness and sagaciousness disarmed the cruel Sisera. While he slept, Heber's wife acted out the prediction, which brought deliverance to God's people. "So God subdued on that day Jabin the king of Canaan before the children of Israel" (verse 23). Through this "mother in Israel" (Judges 5:7) God wrought a great victory. Then Deborah broke out in the song registered in Judges 5. In her praise she said, "Blessed above women shall Jael the wife of Heber the Kenite be, blessed shall she be above women in the tent" (verse 24).

Here the Lord used two women: one, well known; the other, ordinary. God used both to demonstrate that He is not beholden to men to accomplish His will. He can deliver with the high or with the low, with the meek, the weak, and the lowly. He is not limited. It is He who gives the victory to those who trust in Him, and by doing so, He humbles the proud.

It is of special note that in both the books of Kings and Chronicles there is registered the phrase "his mother's name" more than 25 times (e.g., 1 Kings 14:21, 31; 2 Kings 12:1). One scribe writes, "And he did evil in the sight of the Lord, and walked in the way of his father, and in the way of his mother" (1 Kings 22:52). Another states, "And his mother's name was Jerusha, the daughter of Zadok. And he did that which was right in the sight of the Lord" (2 Kings 15:33, 34). No other information is written about these women—no other title is mentioned, no accomplishments registered other than the powerful influence of being a mother. Whether their sons were good kings or evil persons, the finger seems to point back to the mothers. There is by insinuation an indictment or a positive affirmation depending on work of the mother.

There is Esther, the queen, who risked her own life to spare her people. Apparently she was left an orphan, and as typical among

---

9 *ELLEN G.WHITE, DAUGHTERS OF GOD, P. 36.*

the Jews of those days, the burden of her upbringing rested on her close relative, cousin Mordecai. "And he brought up Hadassah, that is, Esther, his uncle's daughter: for she had neither father nor mother, and the maid was fair and beautiful; whom Mordecai, when her father and mother were dead, took for his own daughter" (Esther 2:7). Here she is introduced into the annals of history as an orphaned, gorgeous Jewish young woman.

It appears that Mordecai's and other Jewish exile's circumstances contributed to a state of spiritual compromise. For when many returned back to Jerusalem even the priests had intermarried. (See Ezra 10:2-44, Nehemiah 13:23-27.)

It was in this state of affairs that Esther was raised. She and her cousin were apparently strongly Jewish, but nominal in their spiritual commitment, for she did as Mordecai told her and hid her Jewish faith (Esther 2:20). This was unlike Daniel and his three friends (see Daniel chapters 1, 3 and 4) who bravely stood for their faith regardless of the consequences. When the royal decree was pronounced, she was required to enter the beauty contest. The night with the king would determine if she would end up as a mere concubine (Esther 2:13-14) or queen. By providence "the king loved Esther above all the women, and she obtained grace and favour in his sight more than all the virgins; so that he set the royal crown upon her head, and made her queen instead of Vashti" (verse 17).

It was not until the Jews were threatened with extermination that this young woman was forced to make a choice. Would she continue in her nominal state or risk all and take a stand for the right? The situation demanded instant action (see Esther 4:4-8). Mordecai's words imply that there was need to arouse Esther. The language suggests an ultimatum, "Think not with thyself that thou shalt escape in the king's house, more than all the Jews. For if thou altogether holdest thy peace at this time, then shall there enlargement and deliverance arise to the Jews from another place; but thou and thy father's house shall be destroyed: and who knoweth whether thou art come to the kingdom for such a time as this?" (verses 13, 14).

These words jolted her into reality. If she were to save her people, she could no longer conceal her religion and true identity. It is from this moment on that Esther's starry brilliance shines. Her resolute purpose - demonstrated by genuine faith, prayer, and fasting - leaves for all a testimony that anyone can retract their lukewarm condition and stand firm for what is right even if it means the risk of life. Esther demonstrates the truth that there are many in high positions that when brought to the test need not buckle under the pressure for self-survival. Instead, they can come up to the help of the Lord in "such a time as this." Her life's testimony speaks volumes that there is hope for those who in tough situations may be noncommittal. Yet even if they find themselves in a compromising condition God can still work through them.

In the eleventh chapter of Hebrews, that great Hall of Faith chapter, are found great people of faith, including Sarah, the harlot Rahab, and "women [who] received their dead raised to life again" (Hebrews 11:35), perhaps referring to the Shunammite woman (2 Kings 4:35-37) and the widow of Zarephath (1 King 17:17-24).

Who can deny the great honor bestowed on Mary, the mother of our Lord? No name stands out among women like the name of Mary. "Mary was no doubt chosen primarily because at the appointed time (Dan. 9:24-27; Mark 1:15; Gal. 4:4) her character more closely reflected the divine ideals of motherhood than that of any other daughter of David. She was one of that select minority who were 'waiting for the consolation of Israel' (Luke 2:25, 38; Mark 15:43; cf. Heb. 9:28). It was this hope that purified her life (cf. 1 John 3:3) and qualified her for her sacred role (PP 308; PK 245; DA 69). Every mother in Israel today may cooperate with Heaven as Mary did (DA 512), and may, in a sense, make of her children sons and daughters of God. See on Luke 2:52."[10]

There was another Mary that had quite the opposite reputation from Mary the mother of Jesus. This Mary was the sister of Martha and Lazarus. "It was that Mary which anointed the Lord with oint-

---

*10 THE SDA BIBLE COMMENTARY, VOL. 5, P. 281.*

ment, and wiped his feet with her hair" (John 11:2). Her reputation was not obscured to those who knew her. It was during her anointing of Jesus' feet (see Luke 7:37, 38) that the Bible says, "Now when the Pharisee which had bidden him saw it, he spake within himself, saying, This man, if he were a prophet, would have known who and what manner of woman this is that toucheth him: for she is a sinner" (verse 39).

To these unspoken thoughts Jesus said of Mary, "Why trouble ye the woman? for she hath wrought a good work upon me. For ye have the poor always with you; but me ye have not always. For in that she hath poured this ointment on my body, she did it for my burial. Verily I say unto you, Wheresoever this gospel shall be preached in the whole world, there shall also this, that this woman hath done, be told for a memorial of her" (Matthew 26:10-13). Think of the mark of respect bestowed upon her. Who can contest the fact that Christ was honoring her above all those present.

All the disciples heard the commendation and command given concerning her, including Judas, who was rankled by the indirect rebuke of Christ's words. Yet when it came to making the selection to replace Judas, the fallen disciple, she did not step forward to claim the position. She was not chosen to replace Judas. The disciples did not consider Christ's commendation as a requirement to consider Mary or any of the other women as candidates for the position.

The Bible record of the Acts of the Apostles furnishes us with women who were used by the Lord in the work of salvation. While they were doing ministry, they were not pastors or elders. Doing ministry is not the same as being a minister. One is a task, the other is an ecclesiastical position. The names of several notable women are registered, such as Lydia, a seller of purple (Acts 16:14), and Priscilla, the wife of Aquila. These women and others played an important role as they supported and followed Christ and cooperated in the work of salvation.

Concerning some of these godly women Paul wrote, "And I entreat thee also, true yoke-fellow, help those women which laboured with me in the gospel, with Clement also, and with other my fellow-labourers, whose names are in the book of life" (Philippians 4:3). To the Romans he wrote, "I commend unto you Phebe our sister, which is a servant of the church which is at Cenchrea: That ye receive her in the Lord, as becometh saints, and that ye assist her in whatsoever business she hath need of you: for she hath been a succourer of many, and of myself also. Greet Priscilla and Aquila my helpers in Christ Jesus" (Romans 16:1-3).

According to Strong's concordance Phebe was "a deaconess of the church at Cenchrea, near Corinth."[11] The word "servant" used here is in the feminine. The SDA Bible Commentary says, "the only NT occurrence of this word in the feminine. The use of this term suggests that the office of 'deaconess' may already have been established in the early Christian church."[12] Succourer, the Greek word for helper, is found nowhere else in the New Testament. Outside the New Testament, it is sometimes used to refer to a patron, a woman who supplied support and funding for worthy causes. Apparently these were women who were influential and who had responded to the labors of the apostles. Luke wrote, "And some of them believed, and consorted with Paul and Silas; and of the devout Greeks a great multitude, and of the chief women not a few" (Acts 17:4).

No doubt, these women "succored" (helped) the workers of the Lord. They were "chief women" and as such could possibly contribute personally and financially to do their part to spread the message of salvation.

Speaking of women's abilities to win souls, Ellen White made several statements:

"Women who are willing to consecrate some of their time to the service of the Lord should be appointed to visit the sick, look after the young, and minister to the necessities of the poor. They should be

---

*11 ENHANCED STRONG'S LEXICON (OAK HARBOR, WASH: LOGOS RESEARCH SYSTEMS, INC., 1995).*

*12 THE SDA BIBLE COMMENTARY, VOL. 6, P. 649.*

set apart to this work by prayer and laying on of hands. In some cases they will need to counsel with the church officers or the minister; but if they are devoted women, maintaining a vital connection with God, they will be a power for good in the church. This is another means of strengthening and building up the church. We need to branch out more in our methods of labor. Not a hand should be bound, not a soul discouraged, not a voice should be hushed; let every individual labor, privately or publicly, to help forward this grand work. Place the burdens upon men and women of the church, that they may grow by reason of the exercise, and thus become effective agents in the hand of the Lord for the enlightenment of those who sit in darkness."[13] Concerning this statement, the following should be noted:

a. *This ministry is part-time. "Women who are willing to consecrate some of their time . . ." Therefore, from the start, it does not seem to be referring to pastoral ministry.*[14]

b. *The work is something other than what the church was already doing. "This is another means of strengthening and building up the church. We need to branch out more in our methods of labor."*[15]

c. *It did not even involve holding a church office in the usual sense of the term. The women should be "appointed." The clause, "In some cases they will need to counsel with the church officers or the minister," may be construed as placing them in a category other than that of church officer, although this is by no means certain. Yet it is clear that they are not equated with "the minister" nor are they being regarded as the officers whose responsibility it is to lead the local congregation.*[16]

"Women who have the cause of God at heart can do a good work in the districts in which they reside. Christ speaks of women who helped him in presenting the truth before others, and Paul also speaks of women who labored with him in the gospel. But how very limited is the work done by those who could do a large work if they would! There are families that have means which they could use for

---

13 *ELLEN G. WHITE, IN REVIEW AND HERALD, JULY 9, 1895.*

14 *101 QUESTIONS ON THE SANCTUARY AND ON ELLEN WHITE AS A WRITER, EXAMPLES OF WORDS AND WORD COPYING, 2.2.*

15 *IBID, 2.3.*

16 *IBID, 2.4.*

God's glory in going to distant lands to let their light shine forth in good works to those who need help. Why do not men and women engage in the missionary work, following the example of Christ?"[17] "There certainly should be a larger number of women engaged in the work of ministering to suffering humanity, uplifting, educating them how to believe - simply to believe - in Jesus Christ our Savior."[18]

"If there were twenty women where now there is one, who would make this holy mission their cherished work, we should see many more converted to the truth. The refining, softening influence of Christian women is needed in the great work of preaching the truth. The Lord of the vineyard is saying to many women who are now doing nothing, 'Why stand ye here all the day idle?' Zealous and continued diligence in our sisters toiling for the spread of the truth would be wholly successful, and would astonish us with its results. Through patience and perseverance, the work must be accomplished. . . . We are lacking in deeds of sympathy and benevolence, in sacred and social ministering to the needy, the oppressed, and the suffering. Women who can work are needed now, women who are not self-important, but meek and lowly of heart, who will work with the meekness of Christ wherever they can find work to do for the salvation of souls."[19]

"Discreet and humble women can do a good work in explaining the truth to the people in their homes. The Word of God thus explained will do its leavening work, and through its influence whole families will be converted. . . . In the home circle, at your neighbor's fireside, at the bedside of the sick, in a quiet way you may read the Scriptures and speak a word for Jesus and the truth. Precious seed may thus be sown that will spring up and bring forth fruit after many days."[20]

Replete are the pages of Holy Writ with godly women who

---

*17 ELLEN G. WHITE, IN REVIEW AND HERALD, JULY 21, 1896.*

*18 ELLEN G. WHITE, EVANGELISM, P. 465.*

*19 ELLEN G. WHITE, IN REVIEW AND HERALD, JAN. 2, 1879.*

*20 ELLEN G. WHITE, DAUGHTERS OF GOD, P. 103.*

thought it more than an honor to serve the Master in whatsoever lot they were placed. In their lives we find noble examples worthy of emulation, and, contrariwise, mistakes to avoid like the plague. For example, Jezebel's legacy of idolatry and relentless battle against God's established ecclesiastical order—which ultimately contributed to the ruin of a nation and her disastrous end—is an epitome of the baleful evil influence of a woman.

She bequeathed to her daughter Athaliah her cruelty, mercilessness, ruthlessness, unscrupulousness, and godless traits. Athaliah was the daughter of Ahab and Jezebel (2 Chronicles 21:6; 22:1-3). Her infamy is left recorded in the holy pages. The record states, "His mother's name also was Athaliah the [grand] daughter of Omri. He also walked in the ways of the house of Ahab: for his mother was his counsellor to do wickedly. Wherefore he did evil in the sight of the Lord like the house of Ahab: for they were his counsellors after the death of his father to his destruction" (2 Chronicles 22:2-4). Her desire to place herself in a position not afforded to a women left her trail stained with blood, which brought her to a merciless end. What a legacy to leave behind!

What a contrast between the women who were satisfied to allow God's providence to place them where He saw fit, and the women who strove to go ahead of God, or place themselves where God had not ordained. What a disparity between the final ends of each. Both sides have left their influence either for righteousness or wickedness. Both cases testify to the powerful influence of women for good or for ill.

## PRIESTHOOD OF BELIEVERS

The phrase "priesthood of believers" surfaces when the issue of ordaining women is introduced. However, from whence comes this term? I did a search throughout the Bible to find this phrase. I could not find it. Since it is not a biblical term, whence its origin? It is a coined phrase suggested to have biblical roots when in reality its modern application is incongruous with the Scriptures. Some trace it to the reformer Martin Luther. And though it is true that he used the phrase, it was to emphasize that the Catholic practice of the priesthood was contradictory to Bible teaching and practice. He argued that a common individual such as a peasant was just as capable to approach God, as was a priest. Hence, "the priesthood of believers," meaning that every believer has direct access to God.[21]

Some attempt to extrapolate this concept from a verse of Scripture. They argue that the idea comes from verses in the Bible. The actual text they refer to reads as follows: "Ye also, as lively stones, are built up a spiritual house, an holy priesthood, to offer up spiritual sacrifices, acceptable to God by Jesus Christ. . . . But ye are a chosen generation, a royal priesthood, an holy nation, a peculiar people; that ye should shew forth the praises of him who hath called you out of darkness into his marvellous light" (1 Peter 2:5-9).

Peter is taking this concept from the Old Testament where God says to Israel: "And ye shall be unto me a kingdom of priests, and an holy nation. These are the words which thou shalt speak unto the children of Israel" (Exodus 19:6). Again He said, "And to make thee high above all nations which he hath made, in praise, and in name, and in honour; and that thou mayest be an holy people unto the Lord thy God, as he hath spoken" (Deuteronomy 26:19). The question is: What did God mean by this proclamation, and how did Peter apply it?

Did God intend that everybody in Israel—adults and children, male and female - become priests? Since the statement was made to Moses, who in turn told the people, we must ask, What did Moses understand concerning the declaration? When Moses was told by the Lord to convey what he had said to Israel, the record states, "And Moses came and called for the elders of the people, and laid before their faces all these words which the Lord commanded him" (Exodus 19:7). Moses did not gather the entire congregation as at other times. Instead he called and congregated, not all the men in Israel; no, he called only the elders. The title "elders" was masculine

---

21 *HTTP://WWW.MERRIAM-WEBSTER.COM/DICTIONARY/PRIESTHOOD OF ALL BELIEVERS.*

and applied only to male leaders.

Later on after Israel had settled in Canaan, and during the time of the Judges, the title still pertained only to a select group of men. For example, when Boaz was going to settle the matter as to the right of the next of kin as pertaining to Ruth, the Scriptures says, "And he took ten men of the elders of the city, and said, Sit ye down here. . . . And I thought to advertise thee, saying, Buy it before the inhabitants, and before the elders of my people" (Ruth 4:2-4). "The elders of a town were probably the heads of the various major family groups. They were responsible for the civil and religious interests of the people who lived there. The "elders" were not necessarily aged men, but men of maturity and experience."[22]

Moses did not call the women and men to tell them what God had just declared. Rather he called for those men considered to be leaders of the people. In doing so, he was carrying out God's divine intention—that the entire nation would be governed, not by a nation having a priesthood that included the entire populace, but rather by selected men who would serve as priests directly guided by Him.

The next question is, What did God intend would be the makeup of this priesthood? How would He demonstrate or make concrete the interpretation of this declaration?

The Lord rendered the interpretation of this declaration when He said: "And thou shalt put upon Aaron the holy garments, and anoint him, and sanctify him; that he may minister unto me in the priest's office. And thou shalt bring his sons, and clothe them with coats: And thou shalt anoint them, as thou didst anoint their father, that they may minister unto me in the priest's office: for their anointing shall surely be an everlasting priesthood throughout their generations" (Exodus 40:13-15). Hundreds of years later, when David was making preparations for the building of the Temple, the perpetuity of Aaron's priesthood was recognized. He set up the order by which the

---

22 *THE SDA BIBLE COMMENTARY, ELLEN G.WHITE COMMENTS,VOL. 2, P. 442.*

sons of Aaron would continue their ministry. "These were the orderings of them in their service to come into the house of the Lord, according to their manner, under Aaron their father, as the Lord God of Israel had commanded him" (1 Chronicles 24:19).

In the New Testament we find an apostolic commentary by Paul concerning the priesthood: "And verily they that are of the sons of Levi, who receive the office of the priesthood, have a commandment to take tithes of the people according to the law, that is, of their brethren, though they come out of the loins of Abraham. . . . If therefore perfection were by the Levitical priesthood, (for under it the people received the law,) what further need was there that another priest should rise after the order of Melchisedec, and not be called after the order of Aaron?" (Hebrews 7:5-11).

It is essential to notice that God Himself gave the interpretation and the meaning to the statement. It is therefore not subject to doubt or conjecture concerning His will. By setting up the tabernacle and its services, then assigning only males to serve as priests, God speaks loud and clear giving a concrete interpretation as to the meaning of the proclamation "a kingdom of priests, and an holy nation."

What then was Peter meaning? It was obviously the practice both in the Old Testament and the New to address the family and nation by its leaders. In the fall of Adam and Eve, God held Adam responsible. "For as in Adam all die, even so in Christ shall all be made alive" (1 Corinthians 15:22). The unanimous consensus in the Bible points to Adam, and not Eve as the one responsible for the fall of mankind. Job said: "If I covered my transgressions as Adam, by hiding mine iniquity in my bosom" (Job 31:33).

Upon his visit to the garden, "the Lord God called unto Adam, and said unto him, Where art thou?" (Genesis 3:9). He was the head of the family (see verses 16-21). The apostle Paul wrote: "For Adam was first formed, then Eve" (1 Timothy 2:13). By this statement he was making it clear that Adam was the leader. "Under God, Adam was to stand at the head of the earthly family, to maintain the principles of the heavenly family. This would have brought peace and happiness.

But the law that none 'liveth to himself' (Romans 14:7), Satan was determined to oppose. He desired to live for self. He sought to make himself a center of influence. It was this that had incited rebellion in heaven, and it was man's acceptance of this principle that brought sin on earth. When Adam sinned, man broke away from the heaven-ordained center."[23]

After the Fall, God said: "Behold, the man is become as one of us, to know good and evil: and now, lest he put forth his hand, and take also of the tree of life, and eat, and live for ever: Therefore the Lord God sent him forth from the garden of Eden, to till the ground from whence he was taken. So he drove out the man; and he placed at the east of the garden of Eden Cherubims, and a flaming sword which turned every way, to keep the way of the tree of life" (verses 22-24).

Take special note that God does not say, "Adam and Eve, where art thou?" or "Behold, the man and the woman," but rather, "Adam" and "the man"! In the fourth commandment God addresses both husband and wife by mentioning only the man (see Exodus 20:8-11). There is no question that God holds the man responsible for the spiritual well-being of the family, and the same was true with the church and with the nation.

In the Hebrew economy there were mothers of Israel and fathers of Israel. Yet, when it came to the transference of family authority or estate, it was always conveyed from the fathers to the sons. The same was true with national rulership or leadership transfer of power from royalty. The scepter was always passed on to the sons. Though David, the king, had sons and daughters (2 Samuel 5:13-16), the throne was succeeded by Solomon, his son. David placed him on the throne because it was ordained of God. The Lord said unto him, "If thy children take heed to their way, to walk before me in truth with all their heart and with all their soul, there shall not fail thee (said he) a man on the throne of Israel" (1 Kings 2:4). The Hebrew word for

---

23 *ELLEN G.WHITE, COUNSELS TO PARENTS, TEACHERS, AND STUDENTS, P. 33.*

man is: iysh {eesh}[24] ('ysh) male in contrast to woman, female.[25]

In Old Testament times the burden of the spiritual rudder was always lodged on the shoulders of the fathers. Whether there were female or male prophets, their role was to convey the counsels of God to the men who were the decision-makers. This was the case with Adam, whom God placed in the responsible role of exercising dominion for all of creation on earth (see Genesis 1:26). He was also given the stewardship of the women and his children (see Genesis 3:16). This responsibility God continued to place on the males and their posterity. Paul wrote, "God, who at sundry times and in divers manners spake in time past unto the fathers by the prophets, Hath in these last days spoken unto us by his Son, whom he hath appointed heir of all things, by whom also he made the worlds" (Hebrews 1:1, 2). Paul's words in this inspired commentary of God's ordained protocol gives evidence not of cultural dictation, but rather His election.

This protocol was consistent. When the Lord sent Moses to communicate with the Israelite slaves in Egypt, he ordered him to go directly to the leadership of the people. The Lord said, "Go, and gather the elders of Israel together, and say unto them, The Lord God of your fathers, the God of Abraham, of Isaac, and of Jacob, appeared unto me, saying, I have surely visited you, and seen that which is done to you in Egypt" (Exodus 3:16). It was God's chosen manner of working through the established chain of command. Families were identified, not from the matriarchal line, but always via the patriarchal vein. Passages such as "These be the heads of their fathers' houses" (Exodus 6:14) revealed the constant emphasis God placed on the parentage from the male gender.

The spiritual condition of the people weighed heavily on the fathers. They were held accountable for the lack of spirituality among their families and nation, or for keeping the people faithfully adhering to the ways of the Lord. Moses said, "Only take heed to thyself, and keep thy soul diligently, lest thou forget the things which thine eyes

---

24 *ENHANCED STRONG'S LEXICON, NUMBER 376.*

25 *ENHANCED STRONG'S LEXICON.*

have seen, and lest they depart from thy heart all the days of thy life: but teach them thy sons, and thy sons' sons. . . . And the Lord commanded me at that time to teach you statutes and judgments, that ye might do them in the land whither ye go over to possess it" (Deuteronomy 4:9, 14). God told it to Moses and Moses taught it to the fathers, who in turn taught it to the sons. But the fathers did not follow through with God's counsels. Speaking to the fathers, King Hezekiah said, "And be not ye like your fathers, and like your brethren, which trespassed against the Lord God of their fathers, who therefore gave them up to desolation, as ye see. Now be ye not stiffnecked, as your fathers were, but yield yourselves unto the Lord, and enter into his sanctuary, which he hath sanctified for ever: and serve the Lord your God, that the fierceness of his wrath may turn away from you. For if ye turn again unto the Lord, your brethren and your children shall find compassion before them that lead them captive, so that they shall come again into this land: for the Lord your God is gracious and merciful, and will not turn away his face from you, if ye return unto him" (2 Chronicles 30:7-9).

This prevalent expectation on the part of God toward the fathers did not unburden the individual from maintaining their own spiritual connection with God, nor from their personal accountability to God. For even when the fathers were not true or held their fidelity to God, He declared that there were yet "seven thousand in Israel, all the knees which have not bowed unto Baal, and every mouth which hath not kissed him" (1 Kings 19:18).

When Solomon's Temple was about to be dedicated, he called for the elders of Israel. "Then Solomon assembled the elders of Israel, and all the heads of the tribes, the chief of the fathers of the children of Israel, unto king Solomon in Jerusalem, that they might bring up the ark of the covenant of the Lord out of the city of David, which is Zion. And all the men of Israel assembled themselves unto king Solomon at the feast in the month Ethanim, which is the seventh month. And all the elders of Israel came, and the priests took up the ark" (1 Kings 8:1-3). Fathers and elders were synonymous terms or titles applicable only for men. But as the adage "as the leaders, so the people" was true then, it is still true today. It was when the men had lost their way with the Lord that the Bible records the terrible indictment: "As for my people, children are their oppressors, and women rule over them" (Isaiah 3:12).

God's expectation of the male gender was also carried into the New Testament era. Christ selected 12 men and placed on them the burden of the church. In turn, when the Lord ascended into heaven, His followers likewise placed the burden of Christ's church on the men, which were set aside to shoulder the burden of maintaining the spiritual life in the home and in the church. When Peter was writing to the "strangers scattered" (see 1 Peter 1:1), he was using the same avenue of communication, as was the practice in those days. He sent the message through "Silvanus, a faithful brother" from the "church that is at Babylon" (1 Peter 5:12, 13). Notice that the subject matter in chapter 2 is addressing the believers in general, but channeling his counsels through the men.

In chapter 3 he splits his counsel and addresses wives in particular, then encourages the husbands not to take advantage of their submission.

Then in chapter 4 he returns to giving general counsel by addressing the congregants through the men. "And above all things have fervent charity among yourselves: for charity shall cover the multitude of sins. Use hospitality one to another without grudging. As every man hath received the gift, even so minister the same one to another, as good stewards of the manifold grace of God. If any man speak, let him speak as the oracles of God; if any man minister, let him do it as of the ability which God giveth: that God in all things may be glorified through Jesus Christ, to whom be praise and dominion for ever and ever. Amen. Beloved, think it not strange concerning the fiery trial which is to try you, as though some strange thing happened unto you: But rejoice, inasmuch as ye are partakers of Christ's sufferings; that, when his glory shall be revealed, ye may be glad also with exceeding joy. If ye be reproached for the name of Christ, happy are ye; for the spirit of glory and of God resteth upon you: on their part he is evil spoken of, but on your part he is glorified. But let none of you suffer as a murderer, or as a thief, or as an evildoer, or as a busybody in other men's matters. Yet if any man suffer as a Christian, let him not be ashamed; but let him glorify God on this behalf" (verses 8-16).

Because the communication came through the male leaders, the sacred responsibility then rested on them to convey these counsels to their congregations faithfully. Then the fathers of households were expected to take up the counsels and bring their families into harmony with them. God laid squarely on the fathers the responsibility of the family. Paul wrote, "Husbands, love your wives, and be not bitter against them. Children, obey your parents in all things: for this is well pleasing unto the Lord. Fathers, provoke not your children to anger, lest they be discouraged" (Colossians 3:19). The apostle John also wrote, "I write unto you, fathers, because ye have known him that is from the beginning. I write unto you, young men, because ye have overcome the wicked one. I write unto you, little children, because ye have known the Father. I have written unto you, fathers, because ye have known him that is from the beginning" (1 John 2:13, 14). Once again, the flow of responsibility for the collective spiritual climate of the family was placed on the men.

It would have been highly unlikely for the apostle Peter to bypass the men or elders of the churches and write to the wives, or for women to give advice to the men. That is why he wrote in chapter 5, "The elders which are among you I exhort, who am also an elder, and a witness of the sufferings of Christ, and also a partaker of the glory that shall be revealed" (verse 1). It is only the apostle John who writes a personal pastoral letter to the "elect lady" (see 2 John). Unlike the other letters, this one apparently was written to a single mother encouraging her and commending her in maintaining her loyalty to Christ as well as to her children. Otherwise, all counsels sent to the churches were sent to the elders or leaders, and read by them in.the churches. These church leaders were all men. In fact, the very title "bishop" is always applied to the male gender, and never to women.

Concerning this fact Paul writes, "This is a true saying, If a man desire the office of a bishop, he desireth a good work. A bishop then must be blameless, the husband of one wife, vigilant, sober, of good behaviour, given to hospitality, apt to teach" (1 Timothy 3:1, 2). "For a bishop must be blameless, as the steward of God; not self-willed, not soon angry, not given to wine, no striker, not given to filthy lucre; But a lover of hospitality, a lover of good men, sober, just, holy, temperate; Holding fast the faithful word as he hath been taught, that he may be able by sound doctrine both to exhort and to convince the gainsayers" (Titus 1:7-9). "For ye were as sheep going astray; but are now returned unto the Shepherd and Bishop of your souls" (1 Peter 2:25). The same titles of 'Shepherd' and 'Bishop' given to Christ are passed down to the men whom He places as overseers and caretakers of his sheep.

The word "elders" or "elder" is generally used in the New Testament as a title for men leading out in the Christian church. It is used only once when making a contrast between the young women and elder women. Paul, using the term as an adjective, writes: "Rebuke not an elder, but entreat him as a father; and the younger men as brethren; The elder women as mothers; the younger as sisters, with all purity" (1 Timothy 5:1, 2). But all the rest of the time it is used to refer to the male leaders of God's church. For example: "And from Miletus he sent to Ephesus, and called the elders of the church. And when they were come to him, he said unto them, Ye know, from the first day that I came into Asia, after what manner I have been with you at all seasons" (Acts 20:17, 18).

According to Strong's Lexicon (number 1985) a "bishop," from the Greek word episkopos, is defined as an overseer:

*1a) a man charged with the duty of seeing that things to be done by others are done rightly, any curator, guardian or superintendent*
*1b) the superintendent, elder, or overseer of a Christian church*

The word "elders," on the other hand, is used: "among the Christians, those who presided over the assemblies (or churches). The NT uses the term bishop, elders, and presbyters interchangeably."[26]

---

26 STRONG'S ANALYTICAL LEXICON, "ELDERS," NO. 4245.

Paul writes in the succeeding verses, "Let the elders that rule well be counted worthy of double honour. . . . Against an elder receive not an accusation, but before two or three witnesses. Them that sin rebuke before all, that others also may fear. I charge thee before God, and the Lord Jesus Christ, and the elect angels, that thou observe these things without preferring one before another, doing nothing by partiality. Lay hands suddenly on no man, neither be partaker of other men's sins: keep thyself pure" (1 Timothy 5:17-22). "The noun or indefinite pronoun *mēdeni* (no one) is a masculine or neuter dative singular, hence "no man" is a possible translation. The KJV usually translates it "no man" (Matt. 8:4; 9:30; 16:20; 17:9; etc.). Most of the other versions translate "anyone" or "no one."[27] It is important to note here that Paul ordered both Timothy and Titus to ordain elders (presbuteros, 1 Timothy 3:1; Titus 1:5), which were men.

When Korah, Dathan, and Abiram rebelled against Moses, the argument used is precisely the assertion made today—that is, "everyone is now a priest." What was the point of contention? The point of contention was "who had the right or was entitled to be a priest." Notice their rationale. "And they rose up before Moses, with certain of the children of Israel, two hundred and fifty princes of the assembly, famous in the congregation, men of renown: And they gathered themselves together against Moses and against Aaron, and said unto them, Ye take too much upon you, seeing all the congregation are holy, every one of them, and the Lord is among them: wherefore then lift ye up yourselves above the congregation of the Lord?" (Numbers 16:2, 3). They were adamant that "every one of them" "is holy." This language suggests that Korah was paraphrasing the statement God made when He called Israel a "holy nation" (Exodus 19:6).

They also argued that Moses was lifting up himself above the congregation. They might have been sincere. But sincerity does not establish truth. They were sincerely wrong. All had not been called to be priests. God had made His selection. And when they spoke against Moses as supposed advocates for the holiness of the people, in reality

---

27 *E-MAIL FROM GERHARD PFANDL, PH.D. (ASSOCIATE DIRECTOR, BIBLICAL RESEARCH INSTITUTE), FEB. 2, 2014.*

they were in rebellion against God.

Inspiration declares the verdict against the rebels. While some may suppose that these people who were standing up against Moses were rightfully demanding equality, God sees it differently: "They envied Moses also in the camp, and Aaron the saint of the Lord. The earth opened and swallowed up Dathan, and covered the company of Abiram. And a fire was kindled in their company; the flame burned up the wicked" (Psalm 106:16-18). God did not mince words—He called them "wicked"!

Neither Aaron nor Moses urged themselves into the ministry. It was by God's election. Paul wrote, "And no man taketh this honour unto himself, but he that is called of God, as was Aaron. So also Christ glorified not himself to be made an high priest; but he that said unto him, Thou art my Son, to-day have I begotten thee" (Hebrews 5:4, 5). Paul was very clear concerning the sovereignty of God and His authority to be selective. In the book of Romans he wrote, "And not only this; but when Rebecca also had conceived by one, even by our father Isaac; (For the children being not yet born, neither having done any good or evil, that the purpose of God according to election might stand, not of works, but of him that calleth;) It was said unto her, The elder shall serve the younger" (Romans 9:10-12). Once more, as he did when writing to Timothy, Paul here states: "No man taketh this honour."

While it is true that the Greek for "no man" is an "enclitic indefinite pronoun,"[28] which can be translated as "no one," the reference is strictly speaking about Aaron. The priesthood was ordained by God to be carried out by men of God's election. In Timothy, Paul writes, "If a man desire the office of a bishop" (1 Timothy 3:1). Again while the words "a man" can be translated into the words, "whoever or whatever," the requirement of being the husband of one wife quite clearly suggests its translation in this case must be "a man." Obviously, this language precludes women either taking or desiring the title and responsibility of being a bishop.

---

*28 ENHANCED STRONG'S LEXICON. NUMBER 5100.*

What did Peter mean by the statement, "royal priesthood" (1 Peter 2:9)?

To sum up this point, Peter is using the same declaration and analogy of a "royal priesthood, an holy nation" (1 Peter 2:9) from the Old Testament (see Exodus 19:6). The intended purpose was to convey the reality that just as God had chosen Israel to function as a nation under the leadership of the priesthood (that was made up of males), Peter intended for the Gentile churches and all believers to consider themselves in the same relationship with God as ancient Israel. It was the priest who offered sacrifices in the Old Testament and who were to lead in the spiritual matters of Israel. It is in the same sense that God's New Testament church leaders were to hold sacred the spiritual responsibilities of the churches. While all the people are called to be holy, and all are to labor for the Master, it precludes all the believers being pastors or elders. It also omits women as elders. Christ, Paul, Peter, and the rest of the apostles were selective in who could be an elder. They understood the standing the church was to have with God and the sacred responsibility that rested on those who desired the office of a bishop.

Nomenclatures changed. In the New Testament the title was replaced from "priest" to "bishop" or "elder," suggesting that the earthly priesthood ended, giving way to the heavenly priesthood of Christ (see Hebrews 7:22-25; 8:1-6), and creating a new order. The church would not be led by "priests" (sometimes referred to as "shepherds"), but rather by "elders," which at times were also referred to as "pastors" or "shepherds." God would be their God, leading a church with consecrated elders as in times past.

Ellen White makes the same application to the Adventist people that Peter made concerning the Christian believers of his day. "Those who have seen the truth and felt its importance, and have had an experience in the things of God, are to teach sound doctrine to their children. They should make them acquainted with the great pillars of our faith, the reasons why we are Seventh-day Adventists—why we are called, as were the children of Israel, to be a peculiar people, a holy nation, separate and distinct from all other people on the face of the earth. These things should be explained to the children in simple language, easy to be understood; and as they grow in years, the lessons imparted should be suited to their increasing capacity, until the foundations of truth have been laid broad and deep.[29]

While she calls the Adventist people a "holy nation" in all of her writings, there is never a hint that all believers are pastors or elders.

## A SOVEREIGN GOD

There is a basic truth that needs to be considered. And that is that God is the one who determines what is holy. He is the one who can set things aside and make them sacred. In Creation He set aside the Seventh day as "holy" (Genesis 2:2-4). It is He who decides which day is holy. To Moses, He commanded, "Put off thy shoes from off thy feet, for the place whereon thou standest is holy ground" (Exodus 3:5). Before this incidence, the wilderness sand was common until God declared it holy. When giving instruction to Moses to erect the tabernacle, its furniture, and the priest's garments, God said, "And the veil shall divide unto you between the holy place and the most holy" (Exodus 26:33). "And thou shalt make holy garments for Aaron thy brother for glory and for beauty" (Exodus 28:2).

It is not left to any human being to declare or make anything holy. In His divine far-reaching wisdom God has reserved that power only for Himself. He directed the order of all things. Each has a divine purpose. That is why Paul wrote the rhetorical question: "Who art thou that repliest against God? Shall the thing formed say to him that formed it, Why hast thou made me thus? Hath not the potter power over the clay?" (Romans 9:20, 21).

In the controversy with Dathan, Korah, and Abiram, the Lord stated through Moses, "The Lord will shew who are his, and who is

---

29 ELLEN G. WHITE, CHILD GUIDANCE, P. 495.

holy; and will cause him to come near unto him: even him whom he hath chosen will he cause to come near unto him" (Numbers 16:5). It is the Creator's prerogative to determine, appoint, or choose whom or what He wants. Of Israel, He said, "Blessed is the nation whose God is the Lord; and the people whom he hath chosen for his own inheritance" (Psalms 33:12). Jerusalem became the capital of Israel because God had determined it thus. It is written, "Jerusalem, the city which the Lord did choose out of all the tribes of Israel, to put his name there" (1 Kings 14:21).

God is God, and by virtue of that fact, He can exercise His sovereign will at will. This is a divine prerogative only entitled to Him. And because of this prerogative, He could set in motion the plan of salvation to rescue humanity from their ruined and fallen condition. It is He who can turn the current of rivers; who sets up kingdoms and takes them down. To Jeremiah, He said, "See, I have this day set thee over the nations and over the kingdoms, to root out, and to pull down, and to destroy, and to throw down, to build, and to plant" (Jeremiah 1:10).

He determines, and who can say no? "For he spake, and it was done; he commanded, and it stood fast. The Lord bringeth the counsel of the heathen to nought: he maketh the devices of the people of none effect. The counsel of the Lord standeth for ever" (Psalm 33:9-11). To Noah, He said, "I do set my bow in the cloud, and it shall be for a token of a covenant between me and the earth" (Genesis 9:13). What He sets in order, only He can change. What He pronounces stands! He declares: "Hear, O heavens, and give ear, O earth: for the Lord hath spoken, I have nourished and brought up children. . . . The ox knoweth his owner, and the ass his master's crib: but Israel doth not know, my people doth not consider" (Isaiah 1:2).

In the final analysis, when the Lord sets His judgment, He will judge on the basis of what He ordained. His punishment will be meted out to those who have refused to do as he commanded, who have taken that which He declares holy and makes it common, who under the guise of "seeking to please God," "hath changed my judgments into wickedness" (Ezekiel 5:6), who "transgressed the laws, changed the ordinance, broken the everlasting covenant" (Isaiah 5:6), and "who changed the truth of God" (Romans 1:25). The strongest denunciations inscribed in the Bible are against those who have added to, or changed, His counsels by mixing His truths with error, and by it, causing the whole world to become drunk (see Revelation 14:9-11; 22:18, 19).

Fearful are the warnings laid out in Holy Writ for those who dabble and alter that which the Lord Himself has established. We are told: "Let us hear the conclusion of the whole matter: Fear God, and keep his commandments: for this is the whole duty of man. For God shall bring every work into judgment, with every secret thing, whether it be good, or whether it be evil" (Ecclesiastes 12:13, 14).

The indictment against God's people in those days was: "Her priests have violated my law, and have profaned mine holy things: they have put no difference between the holy and profane, neither have they shewed difference between the unclean and the clean, and have hid their eyes from my sabbaths, and I am profaned among them" (Ezekiel 22:26). The amalgamation of truth with error, or the substitution of that which the Lord had established or ordained with something else, was a serious offense. Their actions were contrary to the injunction to "teach my people the difference between the holy and profane, and cause them to discern between the unclean and the clean" (Ezekiel 44:23).

It is from the Bible that people learn to differentiate between the clean and the unclean. It is in its sacred pages that we discover what God considers holy and that which is unholy. It is there that we learn the difference between what is right and what is wrong. It is the only safe standard of measurement. To veer off from the Scriptures is to cause the people to become confused. To suggest that to achieve peace the Scriptures need to be sidestepped is to create a downward spiral whose currents will be impossible to stop or reverse. The servant of the Lord wrote: "We cannot purchase peace and unity by sacrificing the truth. The conflict may be long and painful, but at any cost we must hold fast the word of God."[30]

## UNSANCTIFIED INTRUSIONS

The priesthood in the Old Testament was a holy position ordained only by God. Its sacredness was highly guarded. There is enough evidence in the Scriptures that precludes just anyone from entering into the priesthood. Since the Lord had ordained that only men from the Levitical line, and particularly from Aaron's posterity, could be candidates, then the qualifications were extremely limited.

Those not qualified by virtue of the lack of lineage were considered brazen even to dare to self-qualify themselves irrespective of being outside of God's narrow mandate. Let me cite a few examples from the Word. In the biblical record there are some who are registered as urging their way into the ministry, or presumed they were authorized to carry out priestly or ministerial functions. In the Old Testament it was Miriam, Dathan, Korah, and Abiram, plus the 250 princes. Miriam was severely rebuked with leprosy—a living death, for urging herself into a status not of her calling. The uprising and self-promoting of the 250 princes with their leaders into the priesthood was considered rebellion of the worst order requiring extreme consequences. The 250 princes were consumed with fire, and the leadership and families of the rebellion were swallowed up alive by the opening up of the earth. The right as to whom could serve as a priest was so guarded that even after the dispersion of the Jews and the final completion of Jeremiah's prophetic 70-year time period (2 Chronicles 36:20-23, Jeremiah 25:9-12, Daniel 9:2) scrutiny was exercised. The strictest care was employed to ensure that none but those who could prove their lineage would be permitted to perform the rites of the priest in harmony with God's decree. A specific case was registered in the book of Ezra concerning a certain family declaring themselves genuine. "These sought their register among those that were reckoned by

---

30 *ELLEN G. WHITE, HISTORICAL SKETCHES OF THE FOREIGN MISSIONS OF THE SEVENTH-DAY ADVENTISTS, P. 197.*

genealogy, but they were not found: therefore were they, as polluted, put from the priesthood. And the Tirshatha said unto them, that they should not eat of the most holy things, till there stood up a priest with Urim and with Thummim" (Ezra 2:62, 63). In this case, only divine approval was demanded as proof.

King Saul's insubordinate act of making an offering of a sacrifice contributed to losing his kingship. In reference to that experience, the record states, "And Saul said, Bring hither a burnt offering to me, and peace offerings. And he offered the burnt offering. And it came to pass, that as soon as he had made an end of offering the burnt offering, behold, Samuel came; and Saul went out to meet him, that he might salute him. And Samuel said, What hast thou done?" (1 Samuel 13:9-11). Saul's response was: "Because I saw that the people were scattered from me, and that thou camest not within the days appointed, and that the Philistines gathered themselves together at Michmash; Therefore said I, The Philistines will come down now upon me to Gilgal, and I have not made supplication unto the Lord: I forced myself therefore, and offered a burnt offering" (verses 11, 12). To this, "Samuel said to Saul, Thou hast done foolishly: thou hast not kept the commandment of the Lord thy God, which he commanded thee: for now would the Lord have established thy kingdom upon Israel for ever. But now thy kingdom shall not continue: the Lord hath sought him a man after his own heart, and the Lord hath commanded him to be captain over his people, because thou hast not kept that which the Lord commanded thee" (1 Samuel 13, 14).

Uzza was "the ancestral head of a family of Nethinim, or Temple servants."[31] His death, resulting from unlawfully touching the ark (see Numbers 1:51; 4:15, 17-20), was a stinging reminder of God's will concerning the ministry (see 1 Chronicles 13:9, 10). David later said, "None ought to carry the ark of God but the Levites: for them hath the Lord chosen to carry the ark of God, and to minister unto him for ever" (1 Chronicles 15:2). Then he said to the heads of the Levites, "Ye are the chief of the fathers of the Levites: sanctify yourselves, both ye and your brethren, that ye may bring up the ark of the

---

31 *HORN, SIEGFRIED H., SEVENTH-DAY ADVENTIST BIBLE DICTIONARY, P 1121.*

Lord God of Israel unto the place that I have prepared for it. For because ye did it not at the first, the Lord our God made a breach upon us, for that we sought him not after the due order" (verses 12, 13). The author of Hebrews makes the strong argument that God's election is axiomatic. He wrote: "And no man taketh this honour unto himself, but he that is called of God, as was Aaron" (Hebrews 5:4).

Jeroboam played the role of the priest. He also appointed of the "lowest of the people priests" (1 Kings 13:33). Jezebel also did the same, as well as her 400 prophets who masqueraded themselves as priests. In both cases, God showed his displeasure. Both ended their lives' journey leaving behind as their posterity degradation, idolatry, apostasy, and national ruin (see 1 Kings 13:1, 2; 18:22-40). Because they were the epitome of rebellion against God, they are specifically named. Jeroboam's name would become proverbial for his idolatrous wickedness (see 2 Kings 3:3; 9:9; 10:29; 13:2, 6, 11; 15:8, 9).

The same is true with Jezebel. "Through the influence of Jezebel and her impious priests, the people were taught that the idol gods that had been set up were deities, ruling by their mystic power the elements of earth, fire, and water. All the bounties of heaven—the running brooks, the streams of living water, the gentle dew, the showers of rain which refreshed the earth and caused the fields to bring forth abundantly—were ascribed to the favor of Baal and Ashtoreth, instead of to the Giver of every good and perfect gift."[32] Jezebel's final end testifies to the detestable state this woman had reached before the Lord. The Lord declared: "And the dogs shall eat Jezebel in the portion of Jezreel, and there shall be none to bury her. . . . And he [Jehu] said, This is the word of the Lord, which he spake by his servant Elijah the Tishbite, saying, In the portion of Jezreel shall dogs eat the flesh of Jezebel: And the carcase of Jezebel shall be as dung upon the face of the field in the portion of Jezreel; so that they shall not say, This is Jezebel" (2 Kings 9:10, 36, 37). Her impenitent, defiant, and rebellious spirit has been inscribed as a warning for generations to come (see Revelation 2:20-23).

---

32 *ELLEN G. WHITE, CONFLICT AND COURAGE, P. 204.*

King Uzziah demonstrated an obstinate, incorrigible attitude of pushing his way into performing acts only permitted by a priest. The record is left for our admonition (1 Corinthians 10:11). The Bible says, "But when he was strong, his heart was lifted up to his destruction: for he transgressed against the Lord his God, and went into the temple of the Lord to burn incense upon the altar of incense. And Azariah the priest went in after him, and with him fourscore priests of the Lord, that were valiant men: And they withstood Uzziah the king, and said unto him, It appertaineth not unto thee, Uzziah, to burn incense unto the Lord, but to the priests the sons of Aaron, that are consecrated to burn incense: go out of the sanctuary; for thou hast trespassed; neither shall it be for thine honour from the Lord God. Then Uzziah was wroth, and had a censer in his hand to burn incense: and while he was wroth with the priests, the leprosy even rose up in his forehead before the priests in the house of the Lord, from beside the incense altar. And Azariah the chief priest, and all the priests, looked upon him, and, behold, he was leprous in his forehead, and they thrust him out from thence; yea, himself hasted also to go out, because the Lord had smitten him" (2 Chronicles 26:16-20).

There is a strange, overpowering sedation that takes over people's minds so that they plunge headlong in an obdurate, blind state into perdition. This is a mysterious enigma. Depressing is the list of those who attempted to displace the priesthood, and the resulting devastating overthrow of each. This is the second time that a person is struck with leprosy for obstinately and presumptuously pressing themselves into the role of the priesthood. The first was Miriam, a woman; the second, a man. Need God speak any louder?

In the New Testament there is one that urged himself into Christ's ministry. Of all the disciples he stands out. His name was Judas Iscariot. "While Jesus was preparing the disciples for their ordination, one who had not been summoned urged his presence among them. It was Judas Iscariot, a man who professed to be a follower of Christ. . . . Judas believed Jesus to be the Messiah; and by joining the apostles, he hoped to secure a high position in the new kingdom. . . . The disciples were anxious that Judas should become one of their number. He was of commanding appearance, a man of keen discernment and executive ability, and they commended him to Jesus as one who would greatly assist Him in His work. . . . The after history of Judas would show them the danger of allowing any worldly consideration to have weight in deciding the fitness of men for the work of God."[33]

## BIBLICAL ORDINATION

Ordination is a topic that is interwoven with the question of women pastors. Perhaps the best place to begin is to ask What is ordination, and who determines and qualifies the candidate? The word "ordination" does not appear in the Old Testament: the word "ordain" or "ordained" does. Its meaning is to "fix," or "found," as in foundation or establish. In the New Testament it appears in Mark 3:14 (Greek: poleo, meaning "do" [357], "make" [113], "bring forth" [14] "commit" [9],[34]) and Titus 1:5 (Greek: kasthistemi, meaning "make" [8], "make ruler" [6], "ordain" [3], "be" [2], "appoint" [1], "conduct [1]"[35]). In Mark, Jesus ordains the disciples. "When Jesus had ended His instruction to the disciples, He gathered the little band close about Him, and kneeling in the midst of them, and laying His hands upon their heads, He offered a prayer dedicating them to His sacred work. Thus the Lord's disciples were ordained to the gospel ministry."[36]

Usually oil was employed in the Old Testament in the anointing ceremony, but its use was not limited to that ceremony. The first registered example of someone dedicating something to God was Jacob's dedication of Bethel. The act of setting things apart by anointing or the pouring of oil was recorded in Genesis 28:18, 19: "And Jacob rose up early in the morning, and took the stone that he had put for his pillows, and set it up for a pillar, and poured oil upon the top of it. And he called the name of that place Bethel."

---

33 *ELLEN G.WHITE, CONFLICT AND COURAGE, P. 285.*

34 *ENHANCED STRONG'S LEXICON.*

35 *IBID.*

36 *ELLEN G.WHITE, THE DESIRE OF THE AGES, P. 296.*

This practice of using oil for consecrating things for a holy purpose was continued into the period when God was personally governing Israel (this period is referred to as the Theocracy). The Levites were thus consecrated with oil. "Then shalt thou take the anointing oil, and pour it upon his head, and anoint him. And thou shalt bring his sons, and put coats upon them" (Exodus 29:7, 8). The actual word "anoint" (in Hebrew, "mashach"[37]) means to smear, or spread a liquid.[38] The laying on of hands was another means of setting aside for a holy purpose. "And thou shalt bring the Levites before the Lord: and the children of Israel shall put their hands upon the Levites: And Aaron shall offer the Levites before the Lord for an offering of the children of Israel, that they may execute the service of the Lord" (Numbers 8:10, 11).

The means of setting aside with oil for a holy purpose was done for kings also, as in the case of Saul. God said: "Tomorrow about this time I will send thee a man out of the land of Benjamin, and thou shalt anoint him to be captain over my people Israel, that he may save my people out of the hand of the Philistines: for I have looked upon my people, because their cry is come unto me" (1 Samuel 9:16). David was likewise anointed (see 1 Samuel 16:13). This setting aside was considered sacred. David considered Saul the "anointed of the Lord" (1 Samuel 24:6) in spite of Saul's actions.

Anointing was also done for separate and distinct offices. The Lord said to Elijah: "Go, return on thy way to the wilderness of Damascus: and when thou comest, anoint Hazael to be king over Syria: And Jehu the son of Nimshi shalt thou anoint to be king over Israel: and Elisha the son of Shaphat of Abelmeholah shalt thou anoint to be prophet in thy room" (1 Kings 19:15, 16). The same olive oil: but completely different and distinct responsibilities. Neither was to cross over - the king was not ordained as a priest; the priest was not ordained as a king. There was only one human being in the entire Bible that held both positions. Only Melchisedec was both king

---

37 *ENHANCED STRONG'S LEXICON, NO. 4886.*

38

and priest. Inspiration declares: "For this Melchisedec, king of Salem, priest of the most high God" (Hebrews 7:1).

The word "anointed" was used in prophetic language concerning the Messiah (see Daniel 9:24-27.) But when Jesus came, He was anointed with the Holy Spirit rather than with oil (see Acts 10:38). Olive oil was a symbol of the Spirit.[39] Paul uses the term to establish his calling. "For all the promises of God in him are yea, and in him Amen, unto the glory of God by us. Now he which stablisheth us with you in Christ, and hath anointed us, is God" (2 Corinthians 1:20, 21).

The manner of setting aside with anointing continued through the Old Testament period. It is not known when this practice ceased. We simply are told that in the New Testament, Jesus used the anointing of oil for the sick (see Mark 6:13). When Jesus called His disciples, He set aside only 12. Many of both genders were following Him, but He chose only men. The Bible record is: "He goeth up into a mountain, and calleth unto him whom he would: and they came unto him. And he ordained twelve, that they should be with him, and that he might send them forth to preach, And to have power to heal sicknesses, and to cast out devils" (Mark 3:13-15).

It is not obvious when the change came in, but Jesus passed on the right of discipleship by laying on of hands, rather than using the oil. Jesus is recorded to lay on hands for healing (see Mark 6:5, Luke 4:40, 13:13). It is assumed that this is the manner that He used for setting apart His disciples, inasmuch as this is the manner that the apostles used to confer authority to the elders and deacons of the Christian churches.

The laying on of hands was practiced in the Old Testament. It was "a ceremony of blessing (Gen. 48:14) and consecration (Num. 8:10), attended and followed by the guidance and wisdom of the Holy Spirit (Deut. 34:9)."[40] It is important to note that although Jacob had

---

39 *ELLEN G. WHITE, CHRIST OBJECT LESSONS, P. 408.*

40 *THE SDA BIBLE COMMENTARY, VOL. 1, P. 923.*

a daughter named Dinah, only the sons were blessed.

"To the Jew, this form was a significant one. When a Jewish father blessed his children, he laid his hands reverently upon their heads. When an animal was devoted to sacrifice, the hand of the one invested with priestly authority was laid upon the head of the victim."[41]

"In the Christian church the laying on of hands in the rite of ordination combines the three aspects of blessing, succession to office, and authority to teach (Acts 6:6; 13:3; 2 Tim. 1:6)."[42]

Once Jesus had ascended, the apostles continued the practice of ordaining as their Lord had given example. During their time of ministry with the Lord, the disciples had witnessed Christ conferring blessings of healing or discipleship by the laying on of hands on multiple occasions (see Matthew 8:3; 9:18; Mark 6:5; Luke 4:40; 13:13; 24:50).

The New Testament churches' practice of setting a person aside for holy use was done by laying on of hands on the candidate. In the book of Acts we see the apostles continue this practice. One text says: "Whom they set before the apostles: and when they had prayed, they laid their hands on them" (Acts 6:6). Paul continued the same practice. "And when they had ordained them elders in every church, and had prayed with fasting, they commended them to the Lord, on whom they believed" (Acts 14:23).

Ordination is vested with authority: "From Christ's ascension to the present day, men ordained of God, deriving their authority from him, have become teachers of the faith. Christ, the True Shepherd, superintends his work through the instrumentality of these

under-shepherds. Thus the position of those who labor in word and doctrine becomes very important. In Christ's stead they beseech the

41 *ELLEN G.WHITE, GOSPEL WORKERS, P. 442.*

42 *THE SDA BIBLE COMMENTARY, VOL. 1, P. 923*

people to be reconciled to God.

The people should not regard their ministers as mere public speakers and orators, but as Christ's ambassadors, receiving their wisdom and power from the great Head of the church. To slight and disregard the word spoken by Christ's representative, is showing disrespect, not only to the man, but also to the Master who has sent him. He is in Christ's stead; and the voice of the Saviour should be heard in his representative."[43]

The Old Testament priests were anointed with oil. And when they were thus set aside, it was with full authority to officiate in that office. "And thou shalt put them upon Aaron thy brother, and his sons with him; and shalt anoint them, and consecrate them, and sanctify them, that they may minister unto me in the priest's office" (Exodus 28:41). "And the holy garments of Aaron shall be his sons' after him, to be anointed therein, and to be consecrated in them. And that son that is priest in his stead shall put them on seven days, when he cometh into the tabernacle of the congregation to minister in the holy place. And thou shalt take the ram of the consecration, and seethe his flesh in the holy place" (Exodus 29:29-31; see also Leviticus 8:29, 30; Numbers 3:3).

The transfer of power from Moses to Joshua was conferred when Moses laid his hands on Joshua. "And Joshua the son of Nun was full of the spirit of wisdom; for Moses had laid his hands upon him: and the children of Israel hearkened into him, and did as the Lord commanded Moses" (Deuteronomy 34:9). This record is registered to authenticate Joshua's authority over Israel. This transfer of power was done in the presence of Israel. "And the Lord said unto Moses, Take thee Joshua the son of Nun, a man in whom is the spirit, and lay thine hand upon him; And set him before Eleazar the priest, and before all the congregation; and give him a charge in their sight. And thou shalt put some of thine honour upon him, that all the congregation of the children of Israel may be obedient. And he shall stand before Eleazar the priest, who shall ask counsel for him after the judgment of Urim

---

*43 IBID*

before the Lord: at his word shall they go out, and at his word they shall come in, both he, and all the children of Israel with him, even all the congregation. And Moses did as the Lord commanded him: and he took Joshua, and set him before Eleazar the priest, and before all the congregation: And he laid his hands upon him, and gave him a charge, as the Lord commanded by the hand of Moses" (Numbers 27:18-23).

When Saul, the first king of Israel, was anointed with oil, he was given authority. "Then Samuel took a vial of oil, and poured it upon his head, and kissed him, and said, Is it not because the Lord hath anointed thee to be captain over his inheritance?" (1 Samuel 10:1). The same is true with David: "So all the elders of Israel came to the king to Hebron; and king David made a league with them in Hebron before the Lord: and they anointed David king over Israel" (2 Samuel 5:3). "I have found David my servant; with my holy oil have I anointed him: With whom my hand shall be established: mine arm also shall strengthen him" (Psalm 89:20, 21). To Solomon, David's son, was transferred the authority and kingly power in the same manner. "And they made Solomon the son of David king the second time, and anointed him unto the Lord to be the chief governor, and Zadok to be priest" (1 Chronicles 29:22).

When Christ called His disciples the record states: "And he ordained twelve, that they should be with him, and that he might send them forth to preach, And to have power to heal sicknesses, and to cast out devils" (Mark 3:14, 15). To this Ellen White wrote, "It was at the ordination of the Twelve that the first step was taken in the organization of the church that after Christ's departure was to carry on His work on the earth. Of this ordination the record says, 'He goeth up into a mountain, and calleth unto Him whom He would: and they came unto Him. And He ordained twelve, that they should be with Him, and that He might send them forth to preach.' Mark 3:13, 14."[44] "As in the Old Testament the twelve patriarchs stood as representatives of Israel, so the twelve apostles stand as representatives of the

---

44 *ELLEN G. WHITE, THE ACTS OF THE APOSTLES, P. 18.*

gospel church."[45]

Paul declares, "Whereunto I am ordained a preacher, and an apostle, (I speak the truth in Christ, and lie not;) a teacher of the Gentiles in faith and verity" (1 Timothy 2:7; see also Mark 3:14). "Their ordination was a public recognition of their divine appointment to bear to the Gentiles the glad tidings of the gospel. Both Paul and Barnabas had already received their commission from God Himself, and the ceremony of the laying on of hands added no new grace or virtual qualification. It was an acknowledged form of designation to an appointed office and a recognition of one's authority in that office. By it the seal of the church was set upon the work of God."[46]

"In the Christian church the laying on of hands in the rite of ordination combines the three aspects of blessing, succession to office, and authority to teach (Acts 6:6; 13:3; 2 Tim. 1:6)."[47]

"Before being sent forth as missionaries to the heathen world, these apostles [including Saul and Barnabas] were solemnly dedicated to God by fasting and prayer and the laying on of hands. Thus they were authorized by the church, not only to teach the truth, but to perform the rite of baptism, and to organize churches, being invested with full ecclesiastical authority."[48] "The Lord employs various instrumentalities for the accomplishment of His purpose, and while some with special talents are chosen to devote all their energies to the work of teaching and preaching the gospel, many others, upon whom human hands have never been laid in ordination, are called to act an important part in soulsaving.

There is a large field open before the self-supporting gospel worker. Many may gain valuable experiences in ministry while toiling a portion of the time at some form of manual labor, and by this

---

45 *ELLEN G. WHITE, GOSPEL WORKERS, P. 445.*

46 *ELLEN G. WHITE, THE ACTS OF THE APOSTLES, P. 161.*

47 *THE SDA BIBLE COMMENTARY, VOL. 1, P. 923.*

48 *ELLEN G. WHITE, GOSPEL WORKERS, P. 441.*

method strong workers may be developed for important service in needy fields."[49]

Take your shoes off, for the ground on which youa re standing is Holy ground.

Election by divine appointment:

Though Reuben was the firstborn, God passed him by and chose Levi for the priesthood. It was God's choice. "And it shall be Aaron's and his sons' by a statute for ever from the children of Israel: for it is an heave offering: and it shall be an heave offering from the children of Israel of the sacrifice of their peace offerings, even their heave offering unto the Lord. And the holy garments of Aaron shall be his sons' after him, to be anointed therein, and to be consecrated in them" (Exodus 29:28, 29). "Bring the tribe of Levi near, and present them before Aaron the priest, that they may minister unto him. And they shall keep his charge, and the charge of the whole congregation before the tabernacle of the congregation, to do the service of the tabernacle" (Numbers 3:6, 7). "And thou shalt take the Levites for me (I am the Lord) instead of all the firstborn among the children of Israel; and the cattle of the Levites instead of all the firstlings among the cattle of the children of Israel" (Numbers 3:41). God set them aside.

This divine choice was later reiterated. The Lord said to Eli, the high priest, who was of the tribe of Levi, "Did I plainly appear unto the house of thy father, when they were in Egypt in Pharaoh's house? And did I choose him out of all the tribes of Israel to be my priest, to offer upon mine altar, to burn incense, to wear an ephod before me? and did I give unto the house of thy father all the offerings made by fire of the children of Israel?" (1 Samuel 2:27, 28). "It is the Lord that advanced Moses and Aaron" (1 Samuel 12:6).

Once more, God reconfirmed the sole calling of Aaron and his sons to the priesthood. "But Aaron and his sons offered upon the

---

49 *ELLEN G.WHITE, THE ACTS OF THE APOSTLES, P. 355.*

altar of the burnt offering, and on the altar of incense, and were appointed for all the work of the place most holy, and to make an atonement for Israel, according to all that Moses the servant of God had commanded" (1 Chronicles 6:49). Before his death, David, by inspiration of the Holy Ghost, confirmed God's appointment of Aaron and his sons to the priesthood. "Aaron was separated, that he should sanctify the most holy things, he and his sons for ever, to burn incense before the Lord, to minister unto him, and to bless in his name for ever" (1 Chronicles 23:13). David then elaborated, with specific language, the ministry to be carried out by these male priests "in the service of the house of the Lord" (verse 32; see also verses 25-31).

After repeated apostasies resulting in shutting down the Temple (2 Chronicles 28:24) by idolatrous kings for more than 300 years between David and Hezekiah, Hezekiah the king reopened the Temple and said to the Levites: "My sons, be not now negligent: for the Lord hath chosen you to stand before him, to serve him, and that ye should minister unto him, and burn incense" (2 Chronicles 29:11). "For so was the commandment of the Lord by his prophets" (verse 25). Biblical revival included restoration of God's true worship, with God's ordained priesthood. There could be no true turning to God without an acknowledgment and a restoration of the divinely appointed order.

It is important to note that when a Levite died without having sons, but only daughters, his passing brought an end to the priesthood of his family. This the Lord made clear when it came to the case of a Levite. The record states, "And Eleazar died, and had no sons, but daughters: and their brethren the sons of Kish took them" (1 Chronicles 23:22). The restatement of his being sonless in 1 Chronicles 24:28 makes a poignant point. It strongly highlights the loss. Though daughters, they were not candidates for the priesthood. His daughters married into the family of Kish and, by doing so, were merged into that family. Here it is clear that God's election of the priesthood was limited only to the male gender. Women were definitely excluded.

God uses repetition to make it certain that He has established the matter and, by so doing, gives it great importance. When Joseph spoke to Pharaoh concerning his dreams, he said to the king, "And for that the dream was doubled unto Pharaoh twice; it is because the thing is established by God" (Genesis 41:32). Therefore, the election of God concerning Aaron and his descendants, being the only ones among a royal priesthood and a holy nation who could be priests, was an ironclad guarantee.

When God elects or ordains, it is not safe to disregard His divine will. When Uzza touched the ark, he died (see 1 Chronicles 13:9, 10). There was divine instruction as to who was qualified, and therefore able to touch, or handle the ark (see Numbers 4:19, 20; cf. Numbers 1:51; 4:15; 7:9). When Saul offered a sacrifice, he was rejected as king (see 1 Samuel 13:11-15). He presumed to offer that which only a priest was ordained to do. When Achan took that which was sacred, he was stoned (see Joshua 7:19-26). When Ananias, with Sapphira, kept a portion that they had consecrated, they died (see Acts 5:1-11).

God determines and establishes the order of things. It is He who has the prerogative of election. David said: "Howbeit the Lord God of Israel chose me before all the house of my father to be king over Israel for ever: for he hath chosen Judah to be the ruler; and of the house of Judah, the house of my father; and among the sons of my father he liked me to make me king over all Israel: And of all my sons, (for the Lord hath given me many sons,) he hath chosen Solomon my son to sit upon the throne of the kingdom of the Lord over Israel" (1 Chronicles 28:4, 5).

Those mentioned above that suffered divine retribution did so because they were presumptuous. They either placed themselves in, or appropriated to themselves, that which they were not elected to be or to do. One of the prevailing sins of our time is that of making common that which is declared to be holy. Or making holy what God considers profane. In either case this spirit or license intentionally veers away from God's directive.

The practice of altering or substituting God's ordained order is a flagrant sin. By this means Satan succeeded in turning the hearts of the people of Israel to other modes of worship. And by doing so, he led them to worship him instead of God. It was this strategy that he used via King Jeroboam to wean away the people from going to Judah where the Temple and its services were. Knowing that their loyalties would remain tied to Judah through the religious activities, he substituted the Levitical priesthood.

The record states, "And Jeroboam said in his heart, Now shall the kingdom return to the house of David: If this people go up to do sacrifice in the house of the Lord at Jerusalem, then shall the heart of this people turn again unto their lord, even unto Rehoboam king of Judah, and they shall kill me, and go again to Rehoboam king of Judah. Whereupon the king took counsel, and made two calves of gold, and said unto them, It is too much for you to go up to Jerusalem: behold thy gods, O Israel, which brought thee up out of the land of Egypt. And he set the one in Bethel, and the other put he in Dan. And this thing became a sin: for the people went to worship before the one, even unto Dan" (1 Kings 12:26-30).

This strategy forced the Levitical priests to abandon Israel and retreat to Jerusalem. "For the Levites left their suburbs and their possession, and came to Judah and Jerusalem: for Jeroboam and his sons had cast them off from executing the priest's office unto the Lord: And he ordained him priests for the high places, and for the devils, and for the calves which he had made" (2 Chronicles 11:14, 15). By this cunning policy of substituting the priesthood, he succeeded in completely replacing the religion of Jehovah with paganism. It was this exact approach that the enemy of souls employed to bring about the substitution of Christ's genuine faith by a human-made religion called the beast, or antichrist. Change or replace the spiritual leadership, and you effectively destroy the genuine.

In heaven God set up a hierarchy. There are seraphims and cherubims. However, all in heaven are satisfied. None desires each other's position. To do so is to repeat the daring of Lucifer to elevate himself to a position designated only for the Creator.

Biblical ordination to pastoral ministry is a God-ordained act of setting men aside for a holy office, and thus conferring on them all ecclesiastical authority. It is a divinely directed mode of election. Throughout the entire Bible all of those set aside by anointing or the laying on of hands were of male gender. While it is true that there were female prophetesses and queens, there is no record that they were anointed. All who were set aside by anointing, ordination, or the laying on of hands were males.

## FINDING FEMININE STRAW

Odd title? Yes, it is true. There is no such thing as feminine straw. Neither is there any such thing in the Bible as a "woman pastor." Yet there are some other verses of Scripture being considered as possible candidates because of the ability to translate them in support of women pastors.

It is being suggested that Rachel, the wife of Jacob, was a pastor. They cite the following verse: "And while he yet spake with them, Rachel came with her father's sheep; for she kept them" (Genesis 29:9). The Living Bible paraphrase reads, "Rachel arrived with her father's sheep, for she was a shepherdess."[50]

The word "shepherd" comes from the word ra`ah[51] in Hebrew. It has several connotations ("feed" [75], "shepherd" [63], "pastor" [8], "herdmen" [7][52]), depending on the context. Those contending for women being ordained suggest this verse proves there were women pastors in the times of the Bible. But stretching this word to this conclusion is the same as saying that the shepherds who drove Jethro's daughters away (see Exodus 2:17), or the 12 sons of Jacob (see Genesis 47:3), or the shepherds that David protected (see 1 Samuel 25:7), or those that kept the sheep during the birth of Christ (see

50 *VERSES MARKED TLB ARE TAKEN FROM THE LIVING BIBLE, COPYRIGHT © 1971 BY TYNDALE HOUSE PUBLISHERS, WHEATON, ILL. USED BY PERMISSION.*

51 *ENHANCED STRONG'S LEXICON, NO. 7462.*

52 *IBID.*

Luke 2:8), were all priests or pastors.

It is true that in the Bible the word "shepherd" is used in terms of men having the oversight or responsibility of looking after God's flock. In the writings of Isaiah, Jeremiah, Ezekiel, and Zechariah the term is used metaphorically of men who serve the people as spiritual pastors or who are unfaithful to their calling of pastors of the people. To cite a few: "His watchmen are blind: they are all ignorant, they are all dumb dogs, they cannot bark; sleeping, lying down, loving to slumber. Yea, they are greedy dogs which can never have enough, and they are shepherds that cannot understand: they all look to their own way, every one for his gain, from his quarter. Come ye, say they, I will fetch wine, and we will fill ourselves with strong drink; and to morrow shall be as this day, and much more abundant" (Isaiah 56:10-12). "And I will set up shepherds over them which shall feed them: and they shall fear no more, nor be dismayed, neither shall they be lacking, saith the Lord" (Jeremiah 23:4). "My people hath been lost sheep: their shepherds have caused them to go astray, they have turned them away on the mountains: they have gone from mountain to hill, they have forgotten their restingplace" (Jeremiah 50:6).

In ordered to determine the intent of the word, the context must be considered. There are many words in different languages that are masculine in nature without a feminine counterpart. For example, in Spanish the word "hammer" is masculine. There is no feminine word for it. In Spanish it is "martillo." And while in Spanish there are masculine and feminine counterparts, there is no feminine for this word. The word "farmer" and "rancher" are also masculine words. If a woman happens to do the work of farming or ranching, she is not called a farmerette, or rancherette. These words do not exist. She would be given the male title of farmer or rancher.

Soldiery and shepherding are tasks normally assigned to men. However, in biblical times, unlike today, only men were soldiers (see 1 Chronicles 7:4, 11; 2 Chronicles 25:5, 6). This was not always the case with the work of shepherds, though most of the time they were males (see 1 Samuel 25:7, 8). When it came to the tasks of taking care of animals, the man's children participated in their care. If a man had only daughters, and he chose the occupation of having sheep or livestock, there was no choice but to have the girls tend to the animals unless he had the means of hiring servants. This was the case with Reuel (Jethro), Moses' father-in-law, who had seven daughters (see Exodus 2:16). But along with having daughters doing the task of shepherding came the burden of bearing with the challenge of not being able to defend themselves against male shepherds, as was the case with Jethro's daughters (see Exodus 2:17). If, per chance, the household had sons and daughters, then all the siblings shared the burden of caring for the animals. This was the case with Rebekah (see Genesis 24:15-20). She rendered "a service which it was customary even for the daughters of princes to perform for their father's flocks and herds."[53] Though she had brothers, she participated in the work of caring for the animals.

To say that Rachel was a pastor because she was referred to as a shepherd would also mean that Jethro, the priest of Median (see Exodus 3:1), had seven pastors. We know that not to be the case, for Jethro is named the only priest in his household (see verse 1). It would mean that the men called shepherds, who drove Jethro's girls away from the well (see Exodus 2:17), were also pastors. It would also mean that all who were called shepherds, as was the case with Jacob's sons (see Genesis 46:32; 47:3), were pastors as well.

The word "shepherd" in those days must have been masculine in nature, because the work of shepherding was typically a man's job. Consequently, if females were forced, because of necessity, to labor in that trade, they were given the male term. It is just like the word "soldier." It is a masculine term. For the military when it comes to decorations of medals for soldiers, the word, importing the masculine gender, includes the feminine.[54] Hence, women being shepherds of flocks of sheep does not translate into their being pastors of men. The Scriptures are clear when using the title "shepherd" to mean animal

---

53 *ELLEN G.WHITE, THE TRUTH ABOUT ANGELS, P. 81.*

54 *HTTP://USCODEBETA.HOUSE.GOV/VIEW.XHTML?REQ=GRANULEID:USC-PRELIM-TITLE10-SECTION3750&NUM=0&EDITION=PRELIM, §3750. SOLDIER'S MEDAL: AWARD; LIMITATIONS ACCESSED JANUARY 25, 2014.*

tenders and when it means pastors of people. In this case it is crystal clear that Rachel was not a pastor of the people - rather, she was a sheepherder.

On many occasions, as an evangelist and as a pastor, I have heard the following arguments: "If the Bible does not forbid it, it must be all right" or "If the Bible does not make mention of it, it must be OK." For example, the smoker argues: "The Bible does not say that you can't smoke, so if God does not specifically forbid it, then I can smoke." Or: "All the commandments are mentioned by Christ except the Sabbath. Therefore, God is not specific about which day to worship on." Another argument says, "The Bible does not say anything about unclean meat in the New Testament. So, don't tell me what to eat."The same rationalization is being used for ordaining women. The argument is "If God does not forbid it, or did not say that it cannot be done, then there is nothing wrong with it."

Needless to say, I was amazed to hear this argument relative to the issue of women pastors. The argument is, "If God does not forbid it, then there is nothing wrong with it." This logic for the support of something on the basis that God is not specific is, to say the least, faulty.

At times God is not specific because it is a foregone conclusion. In other words, the Sabbath is first mentioned in the second chapter of Genesis. It is next mentioned about 1445 B.C.[55] when God intervened in delivering the people of Israel out of Egypt recorded in Moses' writings. This covers a period of about 2,600 years from creation, during which there is no mention of the Sabbath. Since it is not mentioned, does it mean there was no Sabbathkeeping from the time that Christ instituted it until the time of Moses? Obviously, we know that when a speed sign is posted, from the time of notice, until another speed sign is displayed, the original speed limit remains enforced until there is a posted change. That is why God said concerning Abraham: "Because that Abraham obeyed my voice, and kept

---

55 *SDA BIBLE COMMENTARY, VOL. 2, P. 170.*

my charge, my commandments, my statutes, and my laws" (Genesis 26:5).

Though there had not been any mention of written laws from Adam to Moses, it was obvious that not only were God's laws in existence; His followers obeyed them. Like Abraham, who obeyed the statute, commandments, and laws, His children knew the difference between right and wrong. Jacob, knowing it was wrong to deceive, still led his blind father into thinking he was Esau (see Genesis 27) and, by so doing, stole the blessing. This resulted in giving him a tortured conscience and guilt for lying. It was a sin that brought deep and lasting sorrow; he found no peace, neither release of guilt, until he wrestled with the angel. Jacob also knew it was wrong to go before God with strange gods (see Genesis 35:1-4). Joseph knew that it was sin to be morally impure (see Genesis 39:9). God's apparent silence of his laws during the patriarchal times did not leave the transgressor guiltless, nor the obedient ignored.

God's silence on some issues oftentimes is the opposite of the lack of prohibition. On the contrary, it pronounces condemnation for going against or not doing what is intended by the silence. Moses said to the Israelites when God was with them: "Ye heard the voice of the words, but saw no similitude; only ye heard a voice. . . . Take ye therefore good heed unto yourselves; for ye saw no manner of similitude on the day that the Lord spake unto you in Horeb out of the midst of the fire" (Deuteronomy 4:12-15). The absence of any physical description of God was implicit. He intended by the lack of any description to keep them back from idolatry.

In the Bible there is no language that specifically says: "You cannot have more than one wife." Yet we know God's will concerning the matter. Not by what He did not say, but by what He did do. He made one man and gave him one wife at Creation (see Genesis 2:21-25; Matthew 19:3-6). In three of the Gospels of the New Testament, pigs are mentioned, but nothing is said that they could not be eaten. In other words, it doesn't say: "You cannot eat pork." It is because of this apparent silence and absence of an implicit command in the New Testament concerning the Levitical prohibition (see Leviticus 11), that most Christians eat pork. Yet there is no mention that Christ ate it. On the contrary, He used pigs and dogs to illustrate a beggarly faith, a backslidden condition, or apostasy (see Matthew 7:6; 8:30-32; Luke 15:15, 16.) The negative use of these unclean animals reinforces the opposite. The silence, rather than negate, actually substantiates what was already established as a principle.

Christ's disciples followed the same manner of teaching. The apostles used unclean animals as lessons of what Christ's followers should not mimic or emulate (Philippians 3:2; 2 Peter 2:22; Revelation 22:15.) These examples conveyed a strong message suggesting by them the obvious opposite or contrary lifestyle or conduct expected of the believers. So, in the absence of a directive not to eat, we follow the obvious, whose silence substantiates—the unchangeable principles of health.

In the days of Christ there were women priests in the Roman and pagan religions. There were also many forms of idolatry. Yet He never made mention of them. Instead He upheld the Jewish religion and its established order as the only true religion (see Matthew 23:1-3; John 4:22; Mark 7:7-13). By His positive assertion of the true faith he confirmed it, and by His silence concerning the pagan religions He negated them. There is no specific prohibition to Christians in the New Testament against going to the amphitheaters or coliseums to view gladiators' fights. Need there be any prohibition spoken? Christ's strong encouragement to do good to others in love would militate against any desire or relish to view such grotesque bloodthirsty barbarous scenes.

When parents train children, they usually say: "Do as I do, and as I say." As children grow up their observations are directed to the actions of their parents. The same is true with animals. The most effective mode of training is to lead the animal in what to do right, rather than what not to do wrong. When I notice chickens coaching the chicks, they teach by doing, leaving what needs not to be done in silence. Therefore, to survive, the chick follows and mimics the parent, learning from what the parent is doing. There are times when one must teach what not to do, such as "Don't play with fire," etc. But most of the time, by focusing on what needs to be learned outspeaks what needs not to be spoken.

Silence does not give license. On the contrary, it is sometimes the strongest language against an action or thought. Throughout the entire Bible there is the constant mention of only men being priests, pastors, or elders. The silence about women pastors or elders is deafening. God established the Sabbath and kept it in Creation (see Genesis 2:1-3). A few millennia later He inscribed it on tables of stone as part of the Ten Commandments (see Exodus 20:8-11). When He became flesh, He went according to His custom, to the synagogue on the Sabbath (see Luke 4:16); then, in the new heaven and the new earth He declares that all flesh will worship Him from one Sabbath to another (see Isaiah 66:22, 23). The apparent silence during the intervals of time coupled with the restoration dictated a continuance of the practice rather then an abrogation of it. Yet, though practically the entire Christian world is keeping Sunday, He never said: "You shall not worship Me on Sunday." Why? As Christians we do what He has done and said, not what He has not done or said. Why does God need to say any more?

Remember this: "The very beginning of the great apostasy was in seeking to supplement the authority of God by that of the church. Rome began by enjoining what God had not forbidden, and she ended by forbidding what He had explicitly enjoined."[56]

## GOD CALLS ALL INTO MINISTRY

That all have been called to labor for the lost is clear from the Scriptures. Jesus said in Mark 16:15, "And he said unto them, Go ye into all the world, and preach the gospel to every creature." It is important to consider the reality that if I read the statement Jesus made, and I believe it, then the call is applicable to me. Hence, all are called to preach. Of course, many shy away from the thought that

---

56 *ELLEN G.WHITE, THE GREAT CONTROVERSY, P. 289.*

God wants them to preach in the formal sense of getting up before a congregation and delivering a sermon. But the English word "preach" found in several texts is actually translated from different Hebrew or Greek words. Notice the list below from Hebrew and Greek:

| | |
|---|---|
| *Isaiah 61:1* | *(basar): to bear good news* |
| *Jonah 3:2* | *(qara): to call, or cry out* |
| *Luke 9:60* | *(diaggello): to carry a message through* |
| *Acts 16:6* | *(laleo): to speak* |
| *Acts 15:21* | *(kerusso): to publish abroad, be a herald* |
| *Colossians 1:8* | *(kataggello): to promulgate, make known* |
| *Revelation 14:6* | *(euaggelizo): to announce good news, (to bring good news, to announce glad tidings)*[57] |

The list of varying connotations of the word bear out that preaching is not more or less than sharing the good news. The ability to "preach" in the biblical sense is the spontaneous desire to share with others. This spontaneity awakens in men and women, adults and children, when Christ has been experienced in the life, resulting in a spiritual awakening. This preaching, or witnessing, can be accomplished by a one-on-one dialogue, in a home sharing a Bible study, by handing out a tract, through the radio or television, by sending a message through the Internet, by talking or texting on the cell phone, through public speaking, by writing and sending a letter, by short wave radio, or by any other means. Preaching the good news in this sense is not limited to gender or age.

Part of the reason why so few believers preach is because of the misconception that preaching is relegated only to those who are qualified to do so. They also have the mistaken idea that preaching has to be accomplished in the formal setting of a church service done by a minister, experienced preacher, or evangelist.

Evangelism. The last word in the list is evangelism. It is considered a spiritual gift. We get the English word from the Greek word euageglizo.[58] This gift, as well as all the others, was intended to give

57 *ENHANCED STRONG'S LEXICON.*

58 *ENHANCED STRONG'S CONCORDANCE.*

effectiveness to the preaching. "This was the purpose for which talents were committed to us according to our ability to trade upon and cultivate these gifts. As we use our powers, we shall increase our ability to use them, and thus be enabled to do the highest kind of service."[59]

Unlike all the other gifts (e.g. evangelism, tongues, miracles, interpretation of tongues, etc.), preaching is not a gift given to a few. It is not mentioned among the lists of gifts. Why? Because it was intended that all would be able to spontaneously, from a heart overflowing with love for Christ, share what and who He is to them. For that reason, all can and should preach.

Though it is the intention of God that all be preachers or be witnesses (Acts 1:8), sadly, some have taken the words of Paul and misconstrued them. They have been used to insist that women not speak in front of the church or teach. But a quick look at those misused verses reveal a different story. Let me cite them:

First Corinthians 14:34, 35: "Let your women keep silence in the churches: for it is not permitted unto them to speak; but they are commanded to be under obedience as also saith the law. And if they will learn any thing, let them ask their husbands at home: for it is a shame for women to speak in the church."

First Timothy 2:11, 12: "Let the woman learn in silence with all subjection. But I suffer not a woman to teach, nor to usurp authority over the man, but to be in silence."

These verses have been used as "gag orders" to keep women from participating in church services. And while it is true that some have used these verses out of a desire to be in harmony with what they thought the Bible was saying, others have done so out of a chauvinistic spirit. In the fourteenth chapter of Corinthians Paul was addressing the pandemonium that was taking place in the worship services of their church. He not only mentioned women keeping silence—he

---

59 *ELLEN G. WHITE, IN THE YOUTH'S INSTRUCTOR, FEB. 6, 1896.*

also said, "Let all things be done unto edifying. If any man speak in an unknown tongue, let it be by two, or at the most by three, and that by course; and let one interpret. But if there be no interpreter, let him keep silence in the church; and let him speak to himself, and to God" (1 Corinthians 14:26-28). He was not only addressing the women; the men were also being chided and told to be quiet because of their disorderly conduct.

In the first text cited, Paul singled out the ones who were married. He encouraged them to ask their husbands at home. In these verses no mention is made of single or unmarried women. Apparently the married women were taking license in their newfound liberties to talk to their husbands in the church service. In those days (as it is today in Jewish services and in some other religions and countries) the men and women were apart. So, to encourage order, Paul gave his counsel. This was the practice when I attended the services at an Orthodox Jewish synagogue in Brooklyn, New York a few years ago. And when I was in Korea, the men sat on one side and the women on the other. The husband did not sit with the wife, neither the wife with the husband. In this situation it would have been most distracting if a woman were to slip over to the men's side to talk with her husband.

Paul in no way felt that women could not participate in church services. In fact, prior to this counsel Paul wrote in 1 Corinthians 11 the following counsel: "Every man praying or prophesying, having his head covered, dishonoureth his head. But every woman that prayeth or prophesieth with her head uncovered dishonoureth her head: for that is even all one as if she were shaven" verses 4, 5). Here he included both genders in the exercise of the gift of prophecy. And obviously, while he was giving counsel concerning the "right way" to prophesy, he nonetheless was addressing both men and women.

With reference to the exercise of this gift Paul very clearly mandated that it be used solely in the church. Here is what he wrote: "Yet in the church I had rather speak five words with my understanding, that by my voice I might teach others also, than ten thousand words in an unknown tongue. . . . Wherefore tongues are for a sign, not to them that believe, but to them that believe not: but prophesying serveth not for them that believe not, but for them which believe. . . . Let the prophets speak two or three, and let the other judge. If any thing be revealed to another that sitteth by, let the first hold his peace. For ye may all prophesy one by one, that all may learn, and all may be comforted" (1 Corinthians 14:19-31).

Paul was personally acquainted with women prophets. Being a student of the Old Testament Scriptures, he was knowledgeable concerning the prophets Miriam, Huldah, and Deborah. And in his travels Luke, writing about a certain journey, wrote: "And the next day we that were of Paul's company departed, and came unto Caesarea: and we entered into the house of Philip the evangelist, which was one of the seven; and abode with him. And the same man had four daughters, virgins, which did prophesy" (Acts 21:8, 9).

In reference to 1 Timothy 2:11, 12, Paul was addressing the issue of women usurping man's position. Then in verse 13 he began with the word "For." In other words, the reason he had the freedom to state the position of the woman in relationship to man was that "Adam was first formed, then Eve" (1 Timothy 2:13). By this means, he was suggesting that this is God's order of the chain of command - man is to be the head of the woman, not woman to be the head of the man.

When it comes to sharing the gospel, both genders are strongly encouraged to discharge their calling. Notice this statement: "Everyone who hears is to repeat the invitation. Whatever one's calling in life, his first interest should be to win souls for Christ. He may not be able to speak to congregations, but he can work for individuals. To them he can communicate the instruction received from his Lord."[60] "The signs of Christ's coming are too plain to be doubted, and in view of these things everyone who professes the truth should be a living preacher. God calls upon all, both preachers and people, to awake."[61] (Emphasis provided.)

---

*60 ELLEN G. WHITE, THE DESIRE OF AGES, P. 822.*

*61 ELLEN G. WHITE, TESTIMONIES FOR THE CHURCH, VOL. 1, P. 260. (ITALICS SUPPLIED.)*

No one is to be exempted from this privilege. Notice this statement: "Every soul who has accepted this truth should make personal efforts for the salvation of friends and relatives and neighbors."[62] "The spirit of Christ is a missionary spirit. The very first impulse of the renewed heart is to bring others also to the Saviour."[63]

During the persecution that broke out in Jerusalem, which resulted in scattering the believers, Luke wrote, "And Saul was consenting unto his [Stephen's] death. And at that time there was a great persecution against the church which was at Jerusalem; and they were all scattered abroad throughout the regions of Judaea and Samaria, except the apostles. . . . Therefore they that were scattered abroad went every where preaching the word" (Acts 8:1-4). Since the statement confirms that all were scattered "except the apostles," then those that went everywhere preaching were the members.

"To everyone who becomes a partaker of His grace the Lord appoints a work for others. Individually we are to stand in our lot and place, saying, "Here am I; send me." (Isaiah 6:8). Upon the minister of the word, the missionary nurse, the Christian physician, the individual Christian, whether he be merchant or farmer, professional man or mechanic - the responsibility rests upon all. It is our work to reveal to men the gospel of their salvation. Every enterprise in which we engage should be a means to this end."[64]

The focus is to make clear that "God could have reached His object in saving sinners without our aid; but in order for us to develop a character like Christ's, we must share in His work. In order to enter into His joy - the joy of seeing souls redeemed by His sacrifice - we must participate in His labors for their redemption."[65]

In Revelation 22:17 it says, "And the Spirit and the bride say,

---

62 *ELLEN G.WHITE, MANUSCRIPT RELEASES,VOL. 1, P. 16.*

63 *ELLEN G.WHITE, THE GREAT CONTROVERSY, P. 70.*

64 *ELLEN G.WHITE, THE MINISTRY OF HEALING, P. 148.*

65 *ELLEN G.WHITE, THE DESIRE OF AGES, P. 142.*

Come. And let him that heareth say, Come. And let him that is athirst come. And whosoever will, let him take the water of life freely." Most of the time when I ask people, and even pastors, to quote this verse, inadvertently they say, "And the Spirit and the bride say, Come. And let him that hear, come!" The word "say" is missed. The point of this verse is to emphasize that those who hear are not only to come, but, once they have responded, to repeat the invitation.

The pen of inspiration, in making a commentary on this verse, wrote, "The words spoken by Jesus Christ are to be repeated by those who believe them. Those who have genuine faith will make it evident by working for souls who are in darkness."[66] "The Savior's commission to the disciples included all the believers. It includes all believers in Christ to the end of time. It is a fatal mistake to suppose that the work of saving souls depends alone on the ordained minister. All to whom the heavenly inspiration has come are put in trust with the gospel. All who receive the life of Christ are ordained to work for the salvation of their fellow men. For this work the church was established, and all who take upon themselves its sacred vows are thereby pledged to be co-workers with Christ."[67]

The winning of souls is enjoined on all the believers. None is to suppose that this work is relegated solely to the ordained minister. To do so is to commit a fatal mistake. And on the other hand just as fatal is to think they have to be an ordained minister in order to do the work of ministry. "Every true disciple is born into the kingdom of God as a missionary. He who drinks of the living water becomes a fountain of life. The receiver becomes a giver."[68]

From the foregoing it is clear that no one needs to have hands laid upon him or her in order to preach the Word and be a soul winner. All are called to do ministry for the salvation of souls. This ministry does not suggest that a person is a minister or pastor. Rather, he or she is to simply do the labor that Christ enjoins upon all believers.

---

66 *Ellen G. White, That I May Know Him, p. 337.*

67 *Ellen G. White, The Desire of Ages, p. 822.*

68 *Ibid., p. 195.*

Notice the following statements:

1. *"Have you tasted of the powers of the world to come? Have you been eating the flesh and drinking the blood of the Son of God? Then, although ministerial hands may not have been laid upon you in ordination, Christ has laid His hands upon you and has said: 'Ye are my witnesses.'"*[69]

2. *"There are many who are laborers together with God whom we do not discern. The hands of ministers have never been laid upon them in ordination for the work; but nevertheless they are wearing the yoke of Christ, and exert a saving influence in working in different lines to win souls to Christ. The success of our work depends upon our love to God and our love to our fellowmen. When there is harmonious action among the individual members of the church, when there is love and confidence manifested by brother to brother, there will be proportionate force and power in our work for the salvation of men. Oh, how greatly we need a moral renovation! Without the faith that works by love, you can do nothing. May the Lord give you hearts to receive this testimony."*[70]

3. *"Aquila and Priscilla were not called to give their whole time to the ministry of the gospel, yet these humble laborers were used by God to show Apollos the way of truth more perfectly. The Lord employs various instrumentalities for the accomplishment of His purpose; and while some with special talents are chosen to devote all their energies to the work of teaching and preaching the gospel, many others, upon whom human hands have never been laid in ordination, are called to act an important part in soulsaving."*[71]

4. *"There is a large field open before the self-supporting gospel worker. Many may gain valuable experiences in ministry while toiling a portion of the time at some form of manual labor, and by this method strong workers may be developed for important service in needy fields."*[72]

5. *"Brethren and sisters, how much work have you done for God during the past year? Do you think that it is those men only who have been ordained as gospel ministers that are to work for the uplifting of humanity? No, no! Every one who names the name of Christ is expected by God to engage in this work. The hands of ordination may not have been laid upon you, but you are none the less God's messengers. If you have tasted that the Lord is gracious, if you know his saving power, you can no more keep from telling this to some one*

---

69 *ELLEN G. WHITE, TESTIMONIES FOR THE CHURCH, VOL. 6, P. 444.*

70 *ELLEN G. WHITE, TESTIMONIES TO MINISTERS AND GOSPEL WORKERS, P. 187.*

71 *ELLEN G. WHITE, WELFARE MINISTRY, P. 63.*

72 *IBID., P. 64.*

*else than you can keep the wind from blowing. You will have a word in season for him that is weary. You will guide the feet of the straying back to the fold. Your efforts to help others will be untiring, because God's Spirit is working in you."*[73]

6. *"You have neighbors. Will you give them the message? You may never have had the hands of ordination laid upon you, but you can humbly carry the message. You can testify that God has ordained that all for whom Christ died shall have everlasting life, if they believe on Him."*[74]

7. *"Let not the work that needs to be done wait for the ordination of ministers. If there are not ministers to take up the work, let men and women of intelligence, with no thought of how they can accumulate the most property, establish themselves in these cities and towns, and lift up the standard of the cross, using the knowledge they have gained in winning souls to the truth."*[75]

8. *"The knowledge of the truth is altogether too precious to be hoarded up, and bound about, and hid in the earth. Even the one talent entrusted by the Master is to be faithfully employed to gain other talents also. Where are the men and women who have been refreshed with rich streams of blessing from the throne of God? Let them ask themselves what they have done to communicate this light to those who have not had like advantages. How will those who have neglected to use their talents stand in the judgment, when every motive will be brought under scrutiny? The heavenly Master has committed to every one of His servants talents. 'And unto one he gave five talents, to another two, and to another one; to every man according to his several ability.'"*[76]

9. *"There are many ways of working for Christ. Human hands may never have been laid on you in ordination, but God can give you fitness for His service. He can work through you to the saving of souls. If, having learned in the school of Christ, you are meek and lowly in heart, He will give you words to speak for Him. Ask, and receive the Holy Spirit. But*

*remember that the Spirit is given only to those who are consecrated, who deny self, lifting the cross and following their Lord."*[77]

---

73 *ELLEN G. WHITE, IN REVIEW AND HERALD, NOV. 24, 1904.*

74 *ELLEN G. WHITE, SPALDING AND MAGAN COLLECTION, P. 372.*

75 *ELLEN G. WHITE, TO BE LIKE JESUS, P. 90*

76 *IBID.*

77 *ELLEN G. WHITE, IN BIBLE TRAINING SCHOOL, MAR. 1, 1912.*

Ordination does not give supernatural power.

"The ordination by the laying on of hands was, at a later date, greatly abused; unwarrantable importance was attached to the act, as though a power came at once upon those who received such ordination, which immediately qualified them for any and all ministerial work, as though virtue lay in the act of laying on of hands. We have, in the history of these two apostles, only a simple record of the laying on of hands, and its bearing upon their work. Both Paul and Barnabas had already received their commission from God Himself; and the ceremony of the laying on of hands added no new grace or virtual qualification. It was merely setting the seal of the church upon the work of God—an acknowledged form of designation to an appointed office."[78]

Both in the Holy Scriptures and the counsels taken from Ellen White's writings, is enjoined on all believers, ordained or not. The mere act of placing hands on a person does not convey supernatural powers. It is the Spirit that gives power. People of themselves do not possess power that can be transferred just by the laying on of hands. Soul winning is not dependent on having someone having been ordained by the laying on of hands, but rather in the connection the individual has with Him who has said, "Follow me, and I will make you fishers of men" (Matthew 4:19).

There were Jewish priests who practiced exorcism and witchcraft. They used the practice of claiming names or using items, supposing that the name or amulet in of itself contained supernatural powers. Luke wrote: "Then certain of the vagabond Jews, exorcists, took upon them to call over them which had evil spirits the name of the Lord Jesus, saying, We adjure you by Jesus whom Paul preacheth. And there were seven sons of one Sceva, a Jew, and chief of the priests, which did so. And the evil spirit answered and said, Jesus I know, and Paul I know; but who are ye? And the man in whom the evil spirit was leaped on them, and overcame them, and prevailed against them, so that they fled out of that house naked and wounded" (Acts 19:13-16).

---

*78 ELLEN G. WHITE, THE STORY OF REDEMPTION, P. 304.*

Simon the sorcerer assumed the same. When he "saw that through laying on of the apostles' hands the Holy Ghost was given, he offered them money, Saying, Give me also this power, that on whomsoever I lay hands, he may receive the Holy Ghost" (Acts 8:18, 19). He "used sorcery, and bewitched the people of Samaria, giving out that himself was some great one: To whom they all gave heed, from the least to the greatest, saying, This man is the great power of God. And to him they had regard, because that of long time he had bewitched them with sorceries" (verses 9-11). In both cases it was made crystal clear that the mere act of laying on of hands, or even using the name of the Lord in and of itself, could not convey or have any supernatural or magical power.

The power is in God. He determines who receives the call, and the level of empowerment. And all this is based on a personal relationship with Him. He chooses the agent and determines how many gifts or the level of power permitted to be exercised, as well as when that power can be utilized.

## THE NAZIRITE VOW

There were occasions during biblical times when men or women took a Nazirite vow. "The Hebrew root means "to separate," "to consecrate," "to dedicate" in a religious or ceremonial sense. The noun nazir means "consecration," "crown" (as a sign of consecration), and refers also to the person consecrated. The fuller expression, "Nazarite unto God" (Judges 13:5, 7), means one fully dedicated to God."[79] The minimum length of time for a Nazirite vow was 30 days. Some chose a double or triple Nazirite vow that entailed 60 or 90 days. Others made a lifetime commitment.[80]

The first recorded vow of a young woman separating herself for the service of God is found in Judges 11. Although not specifi-

79 *THE SDA BIBLE COMMENTARY, VOL. 1, P. 845.*

80 HTTP://WWW.JEWISHENCYCLOPEDIA.COM/ARTICLES/11395-NAZARITE. *ACCESSED SEPTEMBER 16, 2014*

cally mentioned that it was a Nazirite vow, the daughter of Jephthah seems to have taken a similar type of vow. Some scholars' interpretations determine that Jephthah's daughter was offered up as a human sacrifice. A preferable interpretation is that this is the first recorded consecration of a young woman to God. She was willing to sacrifice her life as a normal woman, including forming a home and bearing children, in order to honor her father's vow to the Lord for the great deliverance given him over Israel's enemies.

At the request of the same people who had ostracized him (see verses 4-8), Jephthah, her father, accepted the offered position of being Israel's leader. Sensing that he needed divine assistance, he made a vow. The Bible says: "And Jephthah vowed a vow unto the Lord, and said, If thou shalt without fail deliver the children of Ammon into mine hands, Then it shall be, that whatsoever cometh forth of the doors of my house to meet me, when I return in peace from the children of Ammon, shall surely be the Lord's, and I will offer it up for a burnt offering" (verses 30, 31). Though it appeared to be a rash vow, nevertheless, it was a vow.

When Jephthah returned back home as a conqueror, to his distress, the one who came out of his door was his only child (see verse 34). To this he said, "Alas, my daughter! thou hast brought me very low, and thou art one of them that trouble me: for I have opened my mouth unto the Lord, and I cannot go back" (verse 35). His day of glory was turned to sorrow. But to her credit, her response was noble. "My father, if thou hast opened thy mouth unto the Lord, do to me according to that which hath proceeded out of thy mouth; forasmuch as the Lord hath taken vengeance for thee of thine enemies, even of the children of Ammon. And she said unto her father, Let this thing be done for me: let me alone two months, that I may go up and down upon the mountains, and bewail my virginity, I and my fellows" (verses 36, 37).

After her return, the Scripture records the outcome. The record states: "And it came to pass at the end of two months, that she returned unto her father, who did with her according to his vow which he had vowed: and she knew no man" (verse 39). What does this mean? Scholars are divided on this. It is improbable that Jephthah was not aware of the counsels of God as passed down by Moses. The tabernacle, with its sacrificial services, was in operation, and Jephthah was obviously acquainted with sacrifices and the seriousness of making a vow to God. As a man of God, he was also filled with the Spirit (see verse 29). He was knowledgeable concerning the history of Israel (see verses 15-28). His daughter's response and devotion give clear evidence that she had been raised to fear and love God. Taking everything into account, The SDA Bible Commentary suggests, among various interpretations, the following: "She was secluded from men the rest of her life, in sacred celibacy, in order that all her moments might be dedicated to the Lord, and that there the virgins of Israel went annually to visit her and bewail her fate."[81] The marginal reference of the King James Version uses the word "or" instead of "and" when it says, "and shall surely be the Lord's." In other words, it was an "either . . . or" situation. Therefore, the verse could read, "or surely be the Lord's." With the Word Bible Commentary says, "Jephthah knew that God's law prohibited human sacrifices, and certainly the Lord would not have given victory on the basis of such an offer. Jephthah's daughter was dedicated to serve the Lord at the tabernacle and therefore remained unmarried."[82]

The KJV Bible Commentary sums up its deliberation between both sides of the scholarly argument. Its conclusion is: "A casual reading of the text would seem to imply that her father put her to death; however, a careful comparison of the character of God and His dealings with Israel, and the character of Jephthah, would seem to prefer the idea that she was given in permanent dedication to the Lord's service. As such, she would never have married and would have remained a virgin forever, unable to perpetuate the line of her father."[83]

---

*81 IBID., P. 378.*

*82 WARREN W. WIERSBE, WITH THE WORD BIBLE COMMENTARY [COMPUTER FILE], ELECTRONIC ED., LOGOS LIBRARY SYSTEM, (NASHVILLE: THOMAS NELSON, 1997). © 1991 BY WARREN W. WIERSBE.*

*83 JERRY FALWELL, EXECUTIVE EDITOR; EDWARD E. HINSON AND MICHAEL KROLL WOODROW, GENERAL EDITORS, KJV BIBLE COMMENTARY [COMPUTER FILE], ELECTRONIC ED., LOGOS LIBRARY SYSTEM, (NASHVILLE: THOMAS NELSON, 1997). © 1994.*

The same concept of humans being "offered" is used when referring to the dedication of the Levites. Moses wrote: "And thou shalt set the Levites before Aaron, and before his sons, and offer them for an offering unto the Lord. Thus shalt thou separate the Levites from among the children of Israel: and the Levites shall be mine. And after that shall the Levites go in to do the service of the tabernacle of the congregation: and thou shalt cleanse them, and offer them for an offering" (Numbers 8:13-15). The Hebrew words for "offer" and "offering" are nuwph and t'nuwphah, respectively. It carries with it the sense of waving or wave offering, shake or lift up.[84] It is the same word used when offering up the parts of animals as wave offerings. The phrase used is, "be waved for a wave offering before the LORD" (Leviticus 7:30).

The Hebrews used at least 13 different words that were translated into the English words: "offer," "offering," or "offered." Deborah the prophet used the following expression: "My heart is toward the governors of Israel, that offered themselves willingly among the people" (Judges 5:9). In verses 9 to 11 she asks "various categories of Hebrew citizens to give thanks for those who had helped to put an end to their Canaanite overlords. First of these were the 'governors' or, literally, the 'lawgivers' or 'law enforcers.' These were princes like Barak who risked their lives for Israel's victory. They were men in the government of Israel whose duty it was to stand for law and national order, and on this occasion they showed themselves to be worthy of their trust. Deborah could well call upon the people to thank God for the part such men had played in the defeat of their enemies, the Canaanites."[85] By risking their lives for the service of the Lord, they "offered" themselves. There was a difference in the offering. Among God's people there was an understanding that animals were sacrificed or slain as an offering, while people's sacrifice or offer was for the purpose of living for service.

Another example of total devotion to the Lord is found in

---

84 *ENHANCED STRONG'S LEXICON, NO. 5130.*

85 *THE SDA BIBLE COMMENTARY, VOL. 2, P. 334.*

reference to Amasiah, a warrior. The Hebrew word used is nadab. This word is also used in reference to animal sacrifices. The first meaning is "offered willingly."[86] "And next him was Amasiah the son of Zichri, who willingly offered himself unto the Lord; and with him two hundred thousand mighty men of valour" (2 Chronicles 17:16).[87]

Paul later states, "I beseech you therefore, brethren, by the mercies of God, that ye present your bodies a living sacrifice, holy, acceptable unto God, which is your reasonable service." (Romans 12:1). The word "sacrifice" has been translated from the Greek word thusia. This is the same exact word used in Luke 2:24 when referring to the turtledove offering made by Joseph and Mary after Christ's birth. The same is true in regard to the "sacrifice" in Hebrews 7:27 that refers to both the animal sacrifices in the tabernacle and the ultimate sacrifice of Christ offering Himself. So, rather than being offered as a human sacrifice, it is reasonable to conclude that Jephthah's daughter was consecrated as a living sacrifice unto the Lord.

Prior to this incident, God had given instruction concerning a vow of dedication a person could make to the service of God. This was not a vow to be a priest, for only the sons of the tribe of Levi could be priests. This was an alternative way, which the Lord provided for non-Levites who desired to consecrate themselves to God. Though the Hebrews made various types of vows, this one was unique. It was the Nazirite vow. Moses was directed to write instruction concerning this vow. In the book of Numbers he wrote: "And the Lord spake unto Moses, saying, Speak unto the children of Israel, and say unto them, When either man or woman shall separate themselves to vow a vow of a Nazarite, to separate themselves unto the Lord: He shall separate himself from wine and strong drink, and shall drink no vinegar of wine, or vinegar of strong drink, neither shall he drink any liquor of grapes, nor eat moist grapes, or dried. All the days of his separation shall he eat nothing that is made of the vine tree, from the kernels even to the husk. All the days of the vow of his separation there shall no razor come upon his head: until the days be fulfilled, in

---

*86* *ENHANCED STRONG'S LEXICON.*

*87*

the which he separateth himself unto the Lord, he shall be holy, and shall let the locks of the hair of his head grow. All the days that he separateth himself unto the Lord he shall come at no dead body. He shall not make himself unclean for his father, or for his mother, for his brother, or for his sister, when they die: because the consecration of his God is upon his head. All the days of his separation he is holy unto the Lord" (6:1-8).

Both men and women were permitted to take this vow to become Nazirites. There were three types of Nazirites: a Nazarite for a set time, a permanent Nazirite, and a Samson-like Nazirite. In the Old Testament both Samson and Samuel, the prophet and judge, were Nazirites. Some suggest that Absalom was also one on account of his long hair. Samson and Samuel were both dedicated to serve the Lord from birth (see Judges 13:4, 5; 1 Samuel 1:26-28, respectively). In the New Testament John the Baptist was to be a Nazirite from birth (see Luke 1:13-15). Jesus, on the other hand, was also dedicated to serve God from birth, but not as a Nazirite.

When it came to women Nazirites, The SDA Bible Commentary says: "We have few records of women Nazarites. They would have been expected to meet conditions similar to those enjoined upon men. If a woman was subject to a father or a husband, either one had the authority to annul her vow (ch. 30:3-5). The fact that the mother of Samson was not to drink wine implies that she may have taken a temporary Nazarite vow (Judges 13:4, 5)."[88] Concerning her, it is written: "She may not eat of any thing that cometh of the vine, neither let her drink wine or strong drink, nor eat any unclean thing: all that I commanded her let her observe" (Judges 13:14).

Anna the prophetess attended the dedication of Christ by His parents in the Temple. While it does not specifically state that she had taken the lifelong Nazirite vow, her constancy in the Temple suggests that her commitment to serve in the Temple was for life. Luke wrote: "And there was one Anna, a prophetess, the daughter of Phanuel, of the tribe of Aser: she was of a great age, and had lived with an hus-

---

*88 THE SDA BIBLE COMMENTARY, VOL. 1, P. 845.*

band seven years from her virginity; And she was a widow of about fourscore and four years, which departed not from the temple, but served God with fastings and prayers night and day. And she coming in that instant gave thanks likewise unto the Lord, and spake of him to all them that looked for redemption in Jerusalem" (Luke 2:36-38).

Extrabiblical sources state that "noble persons also, both men and women, took Nazarite vows. Queen Helena was a Nazirite for fourteen (or twenty-one) years (Naz. iii. 6; see Jew. Encyc. vi. 334, s.v. Helena), and Agrippa's sister Berenice was at Jerusalem on account of a Nazarite vow taken before the outbreak of the great war against the Romans (Josephus, "B. J." ii. 15, § 1)."[89]

Though the biblical information is not voluminous on this topic, it seems indicative that women did dedicate themselves to serve the Lord via this vow either for a short duration of time, as Samson's mother, or for of lifetime of service, as seen in probable interpretations of the lives of Jephthah's daughter and Anna the prophet. These women's dedication demonstrated their love and affection for the things of the Lord. But please note that their service was voluntary, and there is no record that they served as a priest in the work of the Temple. This also disproves the notion that women were exempt from religious participation by virtue of culture, custom, or gender.

Provisions were available for women to consecrate either a portion of or their entire lives to the service of the Lord. This is also substantiated by the practices of women who assembled at the door of the tabernacle. "And he made the laver of brass, and the foot of it of brass, of the looking glasses of the women assembling, which assembled at the door of the tabernacle of the congregation" (Exodus 38:8). The Hebrew word for "assemble" is "tsaba." One of the meanings for this word is "to serve (at sacred tent).[90] The same usage is found when referring to the women assembling in Eli's day.

---

*89 HTTP://WWW.JEWISHENCYCLOPEDIA.COM/ARTICLES/11395-NAZARITE. ACCESSED MAY 23, 2014.*

*90 ENHANCED STRONG'S LEXICON, NO. 6633.*

The passage reads: "Now Eli was very old, and heard all that his sons did unto all Israel; and how they lay with the women that assembled at the door of the tabernacle of the congregation" (1 Samuel 2:22). Apparently Eli's unscrupulous sons led some of these women who served at the door of the tabernacle into sin. Nevertheless, here are biblical records of women who chose to be close to the tabernacle and its services. The normal word used when there was a gathering was "qahal (see Numbers 1:18; Joshua 18:1, 1 Kings 8:1) which meant 'to assemble, gather.'"[91] These women appear to have rendered voluntary service for the tabernacle.

Precisely how these women served is not clear. What is unambiguous is whether these women took a vow of service or chose to render service at the sanctuary without taking a vow. They were not exempt from this privilege as they were from other roles or tasks. There is no evidence that they ever took on the specific work of the priests, nor their office. However, like the priests, those taking on the Nazirite vow for life dedicated themselves to God's service. Perhaps, like Samson and John the Baptist, they took on a specific task directed by the Lord. Or, like Anna, they took on the work of "fastings and prayers" (Luke 2:37), prophesying and witnessing as she did concerning Christ. Or perhaps they were simply like "every women that prayeth or prophesieth" (1 Corinthians 11:5) in the Corinthian church.

A perfect example of a very devoted and committed Christian woman was Tabitha, also called Dorcas (Greek, (Mathetria), female disciple (see Acts 9:36-42). "This woman was full of good works and almsdeeds which she did" (verse 36). After she died, the disciples called for Peter. Upon his arrival "they brought him into the upper chamber: and all the widows stood by him weeping, and shewing the coats and garments which Dorcas made, while she was with them" (verse 39). In today's language she took the responsibility of alleviating the physical needs of the poor and helpless. The famed Mother Teresa was a type of Dorcas.

The ability for women either to take the Nazirite vow or

---

*91 ENHANCED STRONG'S LEXICON, NO. 6950.*

simply to commit to serve at the door of the tabernacle was subject to their marital status. Married women were not as free as single women to exercise that choice. As already stated, a married woman's vow could be annulled by her husband. Also, as Paul stated: "There is difference also between a wife and a virgin. The unmarried woman careth for the things of the Lord, that she may be holy both in body and in spirit: but she that is married careth for the things of the world, how she may please her husband" (1 Corinthians 7:34). A widow, such as Anna, could dedicate her entire time to serving the Lord. However, married women have also served the Lord. The Bible mentions Huldah "dwelt in Jerusalem in the college" (2 Chronicles 34:22). "At that time the prophetess Huldah was living in Jerusalem, near the temple."[92] From these two statements it appears that she was involved in pedagogy as well as serving as a prophet while still being the "wife of Shallum the son of Tikvah, the son of Harhas, keeper of the wardrobe" (2 Kings 22:14). There was no lack of room for service.

As in all ages, there were probably a number of single older women. In the book of Numbers it says, "If a woman also vow a vow unto the Lord, and bind herself by a bond, being in her father's house in her youth; And her father hear her vow, and her bond wherewith she hath bound her soul, and her father shall hold his peace at her: then all her vows shall stand, and every bond wherewith she hath bound her soul shall stand. But if her father disallow her in the day that he heareth; not any of her vows, or of her bonds wherewith she hath bound her soul, shall stand: and the Lord shall forgive her, because her father disallowed her" (30:3-5). This verse only addresses a women "in her youth" living in her "father's house." It says nothing about older single women. These single older women, if they chose to and had no one to answer to, could serve at will as volunteers.

One can immediately see from a biblical point of view that there did not lack opportunities for both genders to serve the Lord. God has always provided ways and means for the devoted to employ their time and talents to His cause, be it male or female. Although some, such as the priests, were recipients of tithe, many others vol-

---

92 *ELLEN G. WHITE, DAUGHTERS OF GOD, P. 44.*

unteered or made a lifelong commitment to serve the Lord without the guarantee of financial support. These devotees were financially supported by family members, as in the case of Samuel by Hannah (see 1 Samuel 2:19), or friends, as in the case of those who supported Christ (see Mark 15:40, 41). "He [Christ] went throughout every city and village, preaching and shewing the glad tidings of the kingdom of God: and the twelve were with him, And certain women, which had been healed of evil spirits and infirmities, Mary called Magdalene, out of whom went seven devils, And Joanna the wife of Chuza Herod's steward, and Susanna, and many others, which ministered unto him of their substance" (Luke 8:1-3). "Their [James' and John's] mother was a follower of Christ, and had ministered to Him freely of her substance. . . . Not only Christ, but His disciples also, labored in the cities and villages; and those who had been in the truth longer than the new converts, ministered unto Him of their substance."[93]

## WOMEN AND SPIRITUAL GIFTS

Talents and spiritual gifts can be traced as far back as the time of Genesis. God created humanity and endowed each person with skills. Adam was placed in "the garden of Eden to dress it and to keep it" (Genesis 2:15). Cain apparently was an agronomist, and Abel was a shepherd (see Genesis 4:3, 4). Concerning other talents, we read, "And Lamech took unto him two wives: the name of the one was Adah, and the name of the other Zillah. And Adah bare Jabal: he was the father of such as dwell in tents, and of such as have cattle. And his brother's name was Jubal: he was the father of all such as handle the harp and organ. And Zillah, she also bare Tubal-cain, an instructor of every artificer in brass and iron: and the sister of Tubal-cain was Naamah" (Genesis 4:19-22).

Though, generally speaking, people were given "natural" talents, others also received spiritual gifts. One of the first mentioned is the gift of prophecy. The book of Jude mentions Enoch as being a prophet:

93 *ELLEN G. WHITE, DAUGHTERS OF GOD, P. 70.*

"And Enoch also, the seventh from Adam, prophesied" (Jude 1:14). After that, Noah did the work of a prophet (see Hebrews 11:7; 2 Peter 2:5), warning the antediluvians about the impending destruction.

Had God not created humanity with the natural ability to develop innate skills, there would never have been the varying talents to contribute to life's needs and wants. Both the righteous and the unrighteous are endowed with varying talents and skills. Today there are volumes of books on a multitude of jobs requiring specific skills or talents and aptitudes. That is why some are mechanics, while others are bakers, tailors, carpenters, machinists, computer technicians, musicians, doctors, scientists, etc.

But apart from these natural aptitudes, talents, and skills, God has reserved what He calls "gifts." These gifts are not natural endowments. Instead, they are supernaturally bestowed on a selected few. These abilities are given only to whom He chooses. The apostle Paul wrote, "But all these worketh that one and the selfsame Spirit, dividing to every man severally as he will" (1 Corinthians 12:11).

For example, it was the gift of prophecy that enabled Noah to foretell the future impending doom and prepare an ark of safety. Abraham was also endowed with the same gift. In warning Abimelech, God said, "Now therefore restore the man his wife; for he is a prophet, and he shall pray for thee, and thou shalt live: and if thou restore her not, know thou that thou shalt surely die, thou, and all that are thine" (Genesis 20:7). Abraham's wife Sarah was also miraculously endowed with the ability of giving birth when it was contrary to the usual course of nature (see Genesis 21:1, 2; Hebrews 11:11).

The family of Jacob would not have been preserved if it were not for the supernatural ability given to Joseph to interpret dreams and visions. When he was 17, he was given prophetic dreams (see Genesis 37:5-10). Though at the time his father, Jacob, did not see the fulfillment, he nonetheless "observed the saying" (verse 11). It became evident to Potiphar, Joseph's overseer, that he had special capabilities, because "the Lord God was with him" (Genesis 39:3; verses

1-3, 23). Through the divinely given gift of interpretation (see Genesis 40:8, 9) Joseph was able to interpret the dream of the baker and butler, and by interpreting Pharaoh's dreams he also saved not only his family but also all of Egypt (see Genesis 40-45). Joseph told his brothers, "God sent me before you to preserve you a posterity in the earth, and to save your lives by a great deliverance" (Genesis 45:7).

When God directed Moses to make a sanctuary for Him (see Exodus 25:8), the need of special expertise was in demand. The construction of the tabernacle, with specific materials and detailed instructions found in Exodus chapters 25-29, demanded particular skills and precise workmanship. Since the Israelites were shepherds by trade (see Genesis 46:32-34), and for more than 400 years of slavery were probably masons, they were not equipped for the task. God made provisions for the commission by giving special gifts to selected individuals. Moses wrote, "And thou shalt speak unto all that are wise-hearted, whom I have filled with the spirit of wisdom" (Exodus 28:3).

There were two men in particular who were supernaturally endowed with the aptitude and talents necessary for the tasks. The record states, "And the Lord spake unto Moses, saying, See, I have called by name Bezaleel the son of Uri, the son of Hur, of the tribe of Judah: And I have filled him with the spirit of God, in wisdom, and in understanding, and in knowledge, and in all manner of workmanship, To devise cunning works, to work in gold, and in silver, and in brass, And in cutting of stones, to set them, and in carving of timber, to work in all manner of workmanship. And I, behold, I have given with him Aholiab, the son of Ahisamach, of the tribe of Dan: and in the hearts of all that are wise hearted I have put wisdom, that they may make all that I have commanded thee" (Exodus 31:1-6).

Unlike spiritual gifts, talents or skills of a trade could be passed on to future generations. This is true of the skills God had given to Aholiab. When building Solomon's Temple, it was one of his descendants who was hired to do the special work with metal. "And king Solomon sent and fetched Hiram out of Tyre. He was a widow's son of the tribe of Naphtali, and his father was a man of Tyre, a worker in brass: and he was filled with wisdom, and understanding, and cunning to work all works in brass" (1 King 7:13, 14). "In 2 Chron. 2:14 we are told that Hiram was the son of a woman of Dan. This is correct, for he was a descendant on his mother's side of Aholiab of the tribe of Dan, to whom, hundreds of years before, God had given special wisdom (PK 63)."[94] Once the talents were bestowed upon the recipients, they could be passed on to their posterity.

At times, people have latent talents they may not be aware of. These abilities may have been passed on from father to son or skipped a generation and show up in the third or fourth generation. From among six brothers, I am the only one to have cultivated a musical talent. I never had formal musical instruction or training, but I became a professional musician and performer. Where did the talent come from? It was not until I became knowledgeable of my estranged father's family that I discovered my grandfather to be a guitarist and one of his cousins to be a famous Puerto Rican professional string performer. God-given talents are perpetuating in nature. These include carpenters, musicians, workers of stone, shepherds, etc. These talents or skills are non-gender. Both males and females can inherit musical, as well as other skills or talents. On the other hand, spiritual gifts can be gender-sensitive.

## SPIRITUAL GIFTS ARE NOT INHERITED

There are many spiritual gifts, and they differ in function. Certain supernatural endowments were given to individual recipients and were never passed on to their posterity. However, some gifts were gender-specific. Certain gifts were given to men and never given to women. Samson, for example, had superhuman strength. The Bible says: "And the woman bare a son, and called his name Samson: and the child grew, and the Lord blessed him. And the spirit of the Lord began to move him at times in the camp of Dan between Zorah and Eshtaol" (Judges 13:24, 25). It was the Spirit, subject to

---

*94 THE SDA BIBLE COMMENTARY, VOL. 2, P. 757.*

Samson's obedient faithfulness to his vow, that gave him the extraordinary strength.

When Samson encountered a lion, the Scriptures bear record that "the spirit of the Lord came mightily upon him, and he rent him as he would have rent a kid, and he had nothing in his hand: but he told not his father or his mother what he had done" (Judges 14:6). The entire story of this remarkable gift is registered in Judges 13-16.

Unlike the perpetuating gift of artificer given to Aholiab, Samson's strength was given him only when the Spirit came and rested upon him (see Judges 14:19; 15:14). Once he violated his vow and betrayed his fealty to God with Delilah, Samson lost his strength (see Judges 16:17-19). Divested of his mighty power and having his eyes plucked out, Samson was sentenced to be chained to a grinding millstone and grind the Philistines' corn like an ox. It was not until his repentance that the Spirit gave him his last dose of power, which resulted in the death of many, including his own (see Judges 16:28-30).

Neither prior to, nor through the rest of biblical history is there any record that this gift of superhuman strength was or had been given or passed on to anyone else, including to a woman. Since it was bestowed and not inherited, it would have been just as easy for God to give this extraordinary gift to a woman. No record exists, however, of God conferring this gift to a female, or anyone else for that matter.

Joseph had sons, but there is no mention that they inherited from their father the gift of interpretation of dreams. The wisdom given to Solomon was unprecedented. God said, "Lo, I have given thee a wise and an understanding heart; so that there was none like thee before thee, neither after thee shall any arise like unto thee" (1 Kings 3:12). Solomon's son Rehoboam succeeded his father on the throne. When the first opportunity was given him to exercise wisdom in a delicate national issue, he proved himself completely devoid of wisdom by choosing to follow counsel that irreversibly split off Israel from Judah (see 1 Kings 12:1-19).

Throughout the Old Testament there are several records of spiritual gifts. But they are not found categorized or in a list as they are in the New Testament. The gifts are simply displayed in the actions of the individuals. Unlike in the New Testament, where particular names were given to the gifts, in the Old Testament many are nameless. While some of the miraculous power or miracles are bestowed, other displays are simply God performing them at the permitted command of His chosen servants. At the stretching of Moses' rod the plagues descended on Egypt, the sea was opened and closed, water gushed out of the rock, and battles were won. Through the prayer of Elijah, the rains did not water the earth for three years, and again came down in answer to his prayer. On the other hand, as long as Samson was loyal to God, he was granted the power. The same is true of people such as Joseph and Daniel, who were given the ability to interpret dreams.

The New Testament refers to the gifts in three different books. They are found in Romans 12, 1 Corinthians 12, and Ephesians 4. The complete text of each follows:

1. *"Having then gifts differing according to the grace that is given to us, whether prophecy, let us prophesy according to the proportion of faith; Or ministry, [diakonia] let us wait on our ministering: or he that teacheth, on teaching; Or he that exhorteth, on exhortation: he that giveth, let him do it with simplicity; he that ruleth, with diligence; he that sheweth mercy, with cheerfulness"(Romans 12:6-8).*

2. *"Now there are diversities of gifts, but the same Spirit. And there are differences of administrations, but the same Lord. And there are diversities of operations, but it is the same God which worketh all in all. But the manifestation of the Spirit is given to every man to profit withal. For to one is given by the Spirit the word of wisdom; to another the word of knowledge by the same Spirit; To another faith by the same Spirit; to another the gifts of healing by the same Spirit; To another the working of miracles; to another prophecy; to another discerning of spirits; to another divers kinds of tongues; to another the interpretation of tongues: But all these worketh that one and the selfsame Spirit, dividing to every man severally as he will"(1 Corinthians 12:4-11).*

3. *"And he gave some, apostles; and some, prophets; and some, evangelists; and some, pastors and teachers; For the perfecting of the saints, for the work of the ministry, for the edifying of the body of Christ"(Ephesians 4:11, 12).*

A comparison below shows the existence of several gifts in both Testaments. While some are not mentioned by name in the Old Testament, they nonetheless existed. Notice the comparative list of both Testaments below:

| *OLD TESTAMENT GIFTS* | *NEW TESTAMENT GIFTS* |
|---|---|
| *Tongues: Genesis 11* | *Tongues: Acts 2; 10* |
| *Prophecy: Genesis 20:7; Jeremiah 1:5* | *Prophecy: Matthew 11:7-10; Luke 2:25-38* |
| *Miracles: Exodus* | *Miracles: John 2:11; Acts 2:22; 8:13* |
| *Wonders: Exodus 4:21* | *Wonders: Acts 6:8* |
| *Super Strength: Judges 14; 15* | *Super Strength: Not found* |
| *Healing: 2 Kings 5:1-19* | *Healing: Matthew 4:23; Acts 4:22* |
| *Wisdom: Deut. 34:9; 1 Kings 4:29, 30* | *Wisdom: Mark 6:2; Acts 6:10; James 1:5* |

The gifts named or titled in the New Testament and not in the Old Testament are:

*1. Romans: ministry (the Greek word is diakonia), exhortation. The others mentioned are "giving" and "ruling." "The term [ministry] is often used in the NT in a general sense to include all ministration and office in the Christian church (see Acts 1:17, 25; 20:24; 21:19; Rom. 11:13; 1 Cor. 12:5; 2 Cor. 3:8, 9; 4:1; 5:18; 6:3; 11:8; Eph. 4:12; 1 Tim. 1:12; 2 Tim. 4:5, 11). Sometimes it is used in a special sense of the distribution of relief and attention to physical needs (Acts 6:1; 11:29, where it is translated 'relief'; 12:25; Rom. 15:31; 1 Cor. 16:15; 2 Cor. 8:4; 9:1, 12, 13)."[95] Paul is obviously using it in the sense of service in temporal matters such as the tasks assigned to the seven deacons (see Acts 6).*

*2. Ephesians: apostles, evangelists, pastors, and teachers. The word Apostle means "one who is sent." Isaiah was sent, and so was Jonah (see Isaiah 6:8, 9; Jonah 1:1). Jonah also did the work of an evangelist (see Jonah 3:1-4). Samuel, Elijah, and Elisha taught in the school of the prophets (see 2 Kings 4:38; 6:1-4, and Prophets and Kings, p. 224).*

*3. 1 Corinthians 12: word of knowledge, faith, discerning of spirits, diverse kinds of tongues, and the interpretation of tongues.*

Something to be considered is that in Romans 12 Paul is addressing the male leaders in particular. The possessors of the gifts here mentioned are men. Notice that he begins addressing the "breth-

---

*95 THE SDA BIBLE COMMENTARY, VOL. 6, P. 619.*

ren" and throughout the chapter he is speaking to "every man" who teaches, or rules, etc. It was customary for Paul to write to the male leaders of the churches. He called them elders (see 1 Timothy 5:1,17, 19; Titus 1:5). The same was true with Peter and John (see 1 Peter 5:1; 2 John 1; 3 John 1). John uses the word presbuteros,[96] usually translated "elder," when addressing "the office of a bishop" (1 Timothy 3:1). James uses the same exact word when suggesting whom to call, and the course to take when a believer was sick. His counsel was "Is any sick among you? let him call for the elders of the church; and let them pray over him, anointing him with oil in the name of the Lord: And the prayer of faith shall save the sick, and the Lord shall raise him up; and if he have committed sins, they shall be forgiven him" (James 5:14, 15). Paul uses the word episkope or episkopos, which means "overseer," when addressing any man who desired to be a bishop or who was serving as head of a congregation. He also uses the word presbuteros interchangeably with episkope.

The gifts or roles noted as being given solely to the male gender are:

| | | |
|---|---|---|
| *1.* | *Strength* | *Judges 13-16 (Samson was the only one.)* |
| *2.* | *Priest* | *Exodus 29:30; Leviticus 1:7, 8; 7:6; Numbers 3:3-13* |
| *3.* | *King* | *1 Samuel 11:15; 15:1; 16:1* |
| *4.* | *Bishop* | *1 Timothy 3:1, 2; Titus 1:7; 1 Peter 2:25* |
| *5.* | *Elder* | *Exodus 3:16-18; 24:1; Matthew 15:2; Acts 4:5, 8; 15:6, 22, 23; Titus 1:5, 6* |
| *6.* | *Pastor* | *Isaiah 56:10-12; Jeremiah 2:8; 10:21; 23:1-4; Ezekiel 34:1-23* |
| *7.* | *Healing* | *2 Kings 5:10-14; 20:1, 5, 7-11; Matthew 10:5-8* |
| *8.* | *Miracles* | *Exodus 11:12; 2 Corinthians 12:12* |

While females, such as Miriam (Exodus 15:20), Deborah (Judges 4:4), Isaiah's wife (Isaiah 8:3), Hulda (2 Kings 22:14), and, in the New Testament, Anna (Luke 2:36) and the daughters of Philip (Acts 21:8, 9), were prophets, there is no record that any of them exercised powers of miraculous acts of healing, resurrecting the dead,

---

*96 ENHANCED STRONG'S LEXICON, P. 402.*

cleansing lepers, etc. There are those who may suggest that the gift of "pastor" was not given solely to men. And while it is true that women did the work of being shepherds, they did so only when it came to animals. No mention is made of any woman serving as a shepherd of a flock of people. And when it comes to the gifts of healing and miracles, all the biblical records point only to men doing healing and miracles within the church of God.

It is only outside of the religion of the God of the Scriptures that women performed prodigious works of miracles or divination. The witch of Endor purported to bring up the dead (see 1 Samuel 28:7-13). Jezebel, wife of king Ahab, did witchcraft (2 Kings 9:22). There was also "a certain damsel possessed with a spirit of divination . . . [who] brought her masters much gain by soothsaying" (Acts 16:16).

There was also a little-known prophetess named Noadiah. She is the only one mentioned by name though there were other unnamed prophets siding with her. Nehemiah's prayer was: "My God, think thou upon Tobiah and Sanballat according to these their works, and on the prophetess Noadiah, and the rest of the prophets, that would have put me in fear" (Nehemiah 6:14). It is clear that she was a leader among the prophets she associated with in Jerusalem who opposed Nehemiah. Her great influence caused Nehemiah to ask for God's protection from her. Since she and the other prophets were hired by Tobiah and Sanballat to oppose Nehemiah, she probably was a false prophetess or, like the prophet Balaam, a hired rival. Perhaps she opposed Nehemiah's continued policy of religious segregation and sided with the non-Jewish women who had to separate from their Jewish husbands.[97]

The fact that the Bible is not silent in its mention of women and their endeavors, accomplishments, escapades, trials, victories, and treasons speaks eloquently of their role in biblical history. Yet, like that of men's roles, women also played an important part in the salvation of humanity. Think of it - without the woman bringing forth the Savior of the world, we would have never been heirs of the hope.

---

97 *THE SDA BIBLE COMMENTARY, VOL. 3, P. 418.*

## WOMEN PRIESTS AND THE CULTURE OF THE DAY

Women stepping over into the priesthood were already prevalent among the heathen and pagan religions in the Old Testament. "The highest ecclesiastical power of the Amen temple at Thebes was Shepenupet II, the daughter of King Osorkon III of the Twenty-third Dynasty, called the 'god's wife.' The office of high priestess had already existed for a long time, and was usually held by a princess of royal blood, by way of securing the loyalty of the priesthood of Amen to the ruling house of Egypt."[98]

In ancient Babylon the culture allowed for women to serve as priests. "Women were significantly involved in the religious activities of ancient cultures. Ordinary women held sacred office and participated in religious events. The office of priestess included various responsibilities encompassing religion, philosophy, prophecy, ethics, healing, ritual, writing and scribal duties, temple construction and maintenance, and, in later periods, raising money.

"In the prehistory of the Mediterranean basin, the weight of archaeological evidence favors the importance of women as religious leaders in prepatriarchal, agrarian cultures. The sacred pantheon reflected a society often termed matriarchal and structured around the concept of the mother. Although there is no written documentation to support the contention that women were priestesses and religious leaders, the great abundance of art and artifacts indicates that this was surely the case, as do the conclusions of anthropology, comparative religion, and evidence from Minoan Crete, which reflects this early culture.

"All Asia Minor worshiped a mother goddess, whose names were many. The goddess and her queen-priestesses, warrior-priestesses, and temple servants reigned long over the cultural life of the area.

---

*98 THE SDA BIBLE COMMENTARY, VOL. 2, P. 52.*

The priestess dressed to resemble the goddess she served and was called by the name of the goddess. The education of a priestess included music and dance, memorization and performance of ritual, the rites of purification, and medicine. As representatives of the protectress of animals, children, and seasonal vegetation, priestesses assured the continuance of life. This they did in two ways: by living the life of the goddess through her rituals and through their knowledge of medicine."[99]

"In Sumer and Babylon there is documentary as well as archaeological evidence for women's high status as priestesses. In the Old Babylonian period (second millennium B.C.E.), the daughters of kings and rulers were appointed as moon-priestesses, or priestess of Inanna/Ishtar (called en or entu priestesses). They wore distinctive clothing, which included the same insignia and garments worn by the ruler, and lived within the sacred shrine, having charge of temple management and affairs and performing ritual and ceremonial duties. They were usually unmarried. In ancient Sumer, priestesses (called nin-dingir) had a similar role; these women participated annually in the Sacred Marriage, representing their goddess and thus ensuring fertility and the continuance of life.

"It is most likely that the later idea of 'temple prostitution' arose from the participation of high priestesses in the sacred marriage rituals; however, such participation rather represented an example of sacred sexual service. "Enheduanna, daughter of King Sargon of Akkad (c. 2371-2316 B.C.E.), was a lifelong priestess of the goddess Inanna/Ishtar and the first known woman poet."[100] Naditum priests were forbidden childbearing and served the male gods Marduk and Shamash. They were drawn from the upper levels of society and entered a temple-complex at an early age. "The naditum priestesses

---

99 *HTTP://GEM.GREENWOOD.COM/WSE/WSEPRINT.JSP?ID=ID553. ACCESSED ON JAN. 26, 2014.*

100 *ELISABETH MEIER TETLOW,WOMEN, CRIME, AND PUNISHMENT IN ANCIENT LAW AND SOCIETY: THE ANCIENT NEAR EAST (CONTINUUM INTERNATIONAL PUBLISHING GROUP, 2004). RETRIEVED JULY 29, 2011. MICHAEL ROAF, MESOPOTAMIA AND THE ANCIENT NEAR EAST, (STONEHENGE PRESS, 1992). RETRIEVED JULY 29, 2011. ENHEDUANNA,WIKIPEDIA, THE FREE ENCYCLOPEDIA. ACCESSED MAY 3, 2014.*

brought to the temple rich dowries, which reverted to their families at their death. They were free to use these dowries for capital in business ventures, to lend money at interest, and to leave the temple to take care of their business dealings. Since they did not bear children, they often adopted daughters and could leave their property to female heiresses. There were many lesser female religious functionaries found in temple-complexes, which sometimes housed upward of several hundred women."[101]

While the warnings of the major Old Testament prophets Isaiah, Ezekiel, and Jeremiah were blaring loudly, Israel and Judah were in hot pursuit of idolatry and emulating the customs of the surrounding people. "During the Twenty-first Dynasty (c. 1085-c. 950 b.c.) the high priests of Amen actually ruled as kings of Egypt, and in Jeremiah's time the high priestesses of Amen were royal princesses.[102]

One of the saddest commentaries concerning the kingdom of Judah that contributed to its eventual demise is registered in the days of king Josiah. In his efforts to bring Israel back to their loyalty to God, "he brake down the houses of the sodomites, that were by the house of the Lord, where the women wove hangings for the grove" (2 Kings 23:7). "The fact that such depraved individuals, both men and women, devoted to religious prostitution, were quartered in a house adjoining the Temple is a sad commentary on the moral collapse that had taken place among the professed people of God. The vile and immoral practices here carried on were part of the idolatrous cer

emonial of the times. Ezekiel denounced the 'wicked abominations' carried on in the Temple area in his day (Eze. 8:5-17). The worst infamies of Canaanite nature worship had made their way into the holy Temple of God. Judah could hardly have sunk to lower depths."[103] "Sacred prostitution was part of the debased practices of Canaanite religion (see 1 Kin. 14:24 and also 15:12; 22:46). The horrible thing

---

*101 WOMEN'S STUDIES ENCYCLOPEDIA, REVISED AND EXPANDED EDITION, ED. HELEN TIERNEY (GREENWOOD PUBLISHING GROUP, 1999) VOL. 3, P. 1191.*

*102 THE SDA BIBLE COMMENTARY, VOL. 4, P. 509.*

*103 IBID., VOL. 2, P. 977.*

here is not just that these perverted persons were practicing their trade in Jerusalem, but that they actually had places for their booths in the temple precincts."[104] This is proof that the Jews absorbed similar practices to the customs around them, including female priests in their paganish forms of worship.

During the reign of the Grecian Empire there is abundant evidence that that culture also had its women priests. "The fourth temple to Artemis owed much of its magnificence to Croesus. It is said to have been burned down on the night of the birth of Alexander the Great in 356 b.c. . . . In the time of Alexander the Great the temple was rebuilt, more stately than ever, and came to be considered one of the Seven Wonders of the World. . . . It had its coterie of priests, priestesses, and boy attendants. Children employed in the temple services were given an education, and priests and priestesses were pensioned after the age of 60 (cf. 1 Tim. 5:9)."[105]

The Romans had quite a curious notion. They believed that the fate and endurance of the empire was dependent on women priests called Vestals. "For more than 1,000 years Rome's Vestal Virgins, a group of six hand-picked women, held unparalleled positions of status as some of the city's most senior religious leaders. They had rank and a level of self-government denied to normal women and as priestesses of Vesta they were responsible for maintaining the soul of Rome."[106]

How to become a vestal virgin:

New initiates were chosen by the chief priest for Rome, the pontifex maximus. From the time of Augustus (ruled 27 B.C. to A.D. 14) this post was held by the emperor.

---

*104 EARL D. RADMACHER, GENERAL EDITOR; RONALD B. ALLEN, OLD TESTAMENT EDITOR, NELSON STUDY BIBLE [COMPUTER FILE], ELECTRONIC ED., LOGOS LIBRARY SYSTEM, (NASHVILLE: THOMAS NELSON, 1997).*

*105 THE SDA BIBLE COMMENTARY, VOL. 6, P. 378.*

*106 JANE LUTWYCHE, ANCIENT ROME'S MAIDENS—WHO WERE THE VESTAL VIRGINS? HTTP://WWW.BBC.CO.UK/RELIGION/0/18490233 ACCESSED ON JAN. 26, 2014.*

1. *Initiates had to be of noble Roman birth, between the ages of 6 and 10.*
2. *Both parents had to be alive.*
3. *They had to be free of mental and physical deformity.*
4. *To become a priest of Vesta, initiates had to agree to remain virgins for the duration of their time as a vestal—at least 30 years.*[107]

It was during the Roman rule that Paul visited Athens. As he wandered about the town, he came to Mars' Hill (see Acts 17:22). "If the apostle was standing atop the rocky hill, he looked down upon the temple of Hephaestus to the northwest, and up to the Parthenon that rose above him on the Acropolis. On the height of that larger hill stood the colossal bronze statue of Athena, who was regarded as the tutelary goddess of her beloved Athens. Below the apostle lay the city itself, which was veritably 'full of idols.'"[108]

Luke the physician, who traveled with Paul and wrote the book of Acts (c. A.D. 61-63),[109] cited an incident with a young woman who was demon-possessed (see Acts 16:16-18). In reference to the episode, The SDA Bible Commentary makes the following comment on the phrase "spirit of divination." It says: "That Luke here uses this unusual adjective implies either that this was the way in which the people of Philippi spoke of the girl or that Luke himself recognized in her wild contortions and shrill cries a similarity to the techniques of the priestesses at Delphi."[110]

In Athens the "patron goddess of the Athenians was Athena Polias; hereditary priestesses who presided over her festivals played an important role in the religious life of the community. Athenians celebrated the birthday of Athena, the Panathenea, annually, and every four years honored her with magnificence. During the festival the great statue of Athena in the Parthenon was presented with a new robe, woven by girls between the ages of 7 and 11 and 'chaste

---

*107 DIVINE WOMEN; HANDMAIDS OF THE GODS, WWW.BBC.CO.UK/RELIGION/0/18490233. ACCESSED ON JAN. 26, 2014.*

*108 THE SDA BIBLE COMMENTARY, VOL. 6, P. 350.*

*109 IBID., VOL. 5, P. 664.*

*110 IBID., VOL. 6, P. 330.*

matrons.'"[111]

Evidence abounds in the annuals of history authenticating the truth relating to extrabiblical practices of women in priesthood as has been cited above. They were as present in Christ's time as they were during the apostolic period and beyond. Consequently, the argument that the reason that the church during biblical times did not follow the practice of placing women in priestly roles was based on culture is unfounded and fallacious.

In those days, it can be argued, women were held below the status of men. However, though it is true that the heathen had subjugated their women to positions even lower than the Israelites, yet, they had women priests; while the Israelites permitted a woman priest only when they were in a state of apostasy.

Neither Christ nor His apostles were locked in, motivated by, or made decisions dictated by the customs or traditions of their time. Today these have been exalted by the word "culture." One cannot read Christ's statements or those of the apostles and rest on the erroneous conclusion that the Lord, when it came to religious matters yielded to or worked on the basis of customs. Christ said, "Howbeit in vain do they worship me, teaching for doctrines the commandments of men. For laying aside the commandment of God, ye hold the tradition of men, as the washing of pots and cups: and many other such like things ye do. And he said unto them, Full well ye reject the commandment of God, that ye may keep your own tradition" (Mark 7:7-9). "Thus have ye made the commandment of God of none effect by your tradition" (Matthew 15:6).

Paul wrote, "Beware lest any man spoil you through philosophy and vain deceit, after the tradition of men, after the rudiments of the world, and not after Christ" (Colossians 2:8). And the apostle Peter admonished, "Forasmuch as ye know that ye were not redeemed with corruptible things, as silver and gold, from your vain conversation received by tradition from your fathers" (1 Peter 1:18).

---

*111 HTTP://GEM.GREENWOOD.COM/WSE/WSEPRINT.JSP?ID=ID553. ACCESSED ON JAN. 26, 2014.*

To insinuate that Christ's actions and ministry were dictated by culture is to cast reproach upon His character. This allegation suggests that He could not be supreme in judgment. That principle must give deference to custom or tradition. All this charges Christ of an imbalance that allows for the melding of pagan practices with biblical truths—a practice that paved the way for the great apostasy in the early Christian church and that held sway up to the great Protestant Reformation in Europe. It was not until then that Christianity turned back to sola scriptura, meaning the Bible and solely the Bible.

Christ is the one who linked heaven and earth (Genesis 28:12-15; John 1:51) and through whom inspiration was given to the Spirit to inspire the prophets (Revelation 1:1). His confidence in the Scriptures was so certain that He banked on them to guarantee His genuineness as the True sent of God (see Luke 24:25-27, 40-47). None other could so fulfill the prophecies of the Old Testament so accurately that the probability of fulfilling just 48 of the more than 300 prophecies concerning the Messiah would have been 1 in 10 to the 157th power.[112]

Though there are exceptions (Romans 2:13-16), generally speaking the salvation of the lost depends upon a knowledge of God through the Scriptures (Matthew 28:18, 19; Romans 10:13-15; 2 Timothy 3:15). This necessitates clarity, unmovable principals, unalterable doctrines, and a well-laid-out path for the honest seeker in the Bible. To suggest the contrary is to imply either that God is not capable of protecting His truth; that all the sacrifices of the lives of both men and women through the ages to ensure the survival of the Scriptures was a waste, or that God has left enough room in the Bible for varying doctrines to justify having over 33,000 Christian denominations worldwide.[113] If it is true that the Bible is contaminated by the social, cultural, and historical influences, in addition to the interpretation of the language of the prophets, as some claim, then

---

*112 PETER STONER, SCIENCE SPEAKS, (CHICAGO: MOODY PRESS, 1976), PP. 106-112.*

*113 BARRETT ET AL,VOLUME 1, PAGE 16,TABLE 1-5,* HTTP://WWW.PHILVAZ.COM/APOLOGETICS/A106.HTMHTTP://WWW.PHILVAZ.COM/APOLOGETICS/A106.HTM. *ACCESSED SEPTEMBER 8,2014.*

the Lord would not have said, "Sanctify them through thy truth: thy word is truth" (John 17:17). Nor would He have encouraged the confidence of finding Him by encouraging individuals to "search the scriptures; for in them ye think ye have eternal life: and they are they which testify of me" (John 5:39).

Neither would Paul have written: "For whosoever shall call upon the name of the Lord shall be saved. How then shall they call on him in whom they have not believed? and how shall they believe in him of whom they have not heard? and how shall they hear without a preacher? And how shall they preach, except they be sent? as it is written, How beautiful are the feet of them that preach the gospel of peace, and bring glad tidings of good things!" (Romans 10:13-15). Or "And that from a child thou hast known the holy scriptures, which are able to make thee wise unto salvation through faith which is in Christ Jesus. All scripture is given by inspiration of God, and is profitable for doctrine, for reproof, for correction, for instruction in righteousness: That the man of God may be perfect, throughly furnished unto all good works" (2 Timothy 3:15-17).

Peter stated, "Knowing this first, that no prophecy of the scripture is of any private interpretation. For the prophecy came not in old time by the will of man: but holy men of God spake as they were moved by the Holy Ghost" (2 Peter 1:20, 21). His confident statement would be untruthful. But since the Spirit was the mover, then the inspiration was divinely generated, not culturally contaminated. It was written "for our learning, that we through patience and comfort of the Scriptures might have hope" (Romans 15:4).

Ellen White wrote, "There are some that may think they are fully capable with their finite judgment to take the Word of God, and to state what are the words of inspiration, and what are not the words of inspiration. I want to warn you off that ground, my brethren in the ministry. 'Put off thy shoes from off thy feet, for the place whereon thou standest is holy ground.' There is no finite man that lives, I care not who he is or whatever is his position, that God has authorized to pick and choose in His Word."[114]

"And although we may try to reason in regard to our Creator, how long He has had existence, where evil first entered into our world, and all these things, we may reason about them until we fall down faint and exhausted with the research when there is yet an infinity beyond. We cannot grasp it, so what man is there that dares to take that Bible and say this part is inspired and that part is not inspired? I would have both my arms taken off at my shoulders before I would ever make the statement or set my judgment upon the Word of God as to what is inspired and what is not inspired."[115]

"How would finite man know anything about that matter? He is to take the Word of God as it reads, and then to appreciate it as it is, and to bring it into the life and to weave it into the character. There is everything plainly revealed in God's Word which concerns the salvation of men, and if we will take that Word and comprehend it to the very best of our ability, God will help us in its comprehension."[116]

"Never let mortal man sit in judgment upon the Word of God or pass sentence as to how much of this is inspired and how much is not inspired, and that this is more inspired than some other portions. God warns him off that ground. God has not given him any such work to do."[117]

"It takes all of eternity to unfold the glories and bring out the precious treasures of the Word of God. Do not let any living man come to you and begin to dissect God's Word, telling what is revelation, what is inspiration and what is not, without a rebuke. Tell all such they simply do not know. They simply are not able to comprehend the things of the mystery of God. What we want is to inspire faith. We want no one to say, "This I will reject, and this will I receive,"

---

*114 THE SDA BIBLE COMMENTARY, ELLEN G.WHITE COMMENTS, VOL. 7, P. 919.*

*115 IBID., P. 919.*

*116 IBID.*

*117 IBID.*

but we want to have implicit faith in the Bible as a whole and as it is."[118]

"We call on you to take your Bible, but do not put a sacrilegious hand upon it, and say, "That is not inspired," simply because somebody else has said so. Not a jot or tittle is ever to be taken from that Word. Hands off, brethren! Do not touch the ark. Do not lay your hand upon it, but let God move. It is with His own power, and He will work in such a manner that He will compass our salvation. We want God to have some room to work. We do not want man's ideas to bind Him about.."[119]

The Jews in Christ's day were "unaccustomed to accept God's Word exactly as it reads, or to allow it to be its own interpreter, [so] they read it in the light of their maxims and traditions. So long had they neglected to study and contemplate the Bible that its pages were to them a mystery. They turned with aversion from the truth of God to the traditions of men."[120]

How often have I encountered those who seize on passages of the Scriptures in order to sustain erroneous doctrines or unchristian practices. They will separate them from the context or combine verses that after close scrutiny reveal they support the opposite view. Both as a pastor and church administrator, I've found the task of trying to correct some of these challenges painstaking, to say the least. I shed tears when a close friend became entangled with some "new light," and, despite many prayers and appeals, continued headlong until my friend abandoned even the basic truths found in the Scriptures.

A new approach to Bible interpretation has been recently introduced. The newly coined hermeneutical approach to biblical interpretation is called "principle-based historical-cultural." The North American Theology of Ordination Study Committee just introduced this method. This committee is referred to by the acronym NAD TOSC.

---

*118 IBID.*

*119 IBID., P. 920.*

*120 ELLEN G.WHITE, CHRIST TRIUMPHANT, P. 226.*

It is apparent that the originators of this approach either are not acquainted with the statements just cited from the inspired counsel or are completely subjugating the counsel to this new mode of interpretation, thus making them applicable only to current time and culture. The proponents of the new method "advocate an approach that takes into account the 'trajectory' of Scripture. . . extrapolated so that the trajectory beyond and outside of Scripture can be seen . . . such an approach, even though it might broadly affirm the Bible's inspiration, nevertheless undermines it by characterizing selected portions of Scripture as time- and culture-bound and, therefore, tinged with the author's prejudicial views on such topics, rather than God's thoughts which are valid for all places and all time' (p. 195)."[121]

It is true that words can evolve in their usage. There are times when the exercise of etymology is necessary. A phrase can mean one thing in New York, and have a different connotation in California. Sometimes when it comes to translation from one language into another, there may not be found a precise transliteration. Therefore, at times several words may be necessary to convey the precise sense of the word or phrase into the other language. What is amazing about the Bible's language is the selection of ideas God chose to use whose meaning have easily conveyed, in spite of the 2, 287 languages,[122] the same message.

We have been warned: "Satan hopes to involve the remnant people of God in the general ruin that is coming upon the earth. As the coming of Christ draws nigh, he will be more determined and decisive in his efforts to overthrow them. Men and women will arise professing to have some new light or some new revelation whose tendency is to unsettle faith in the old landmarks. Their doctrines will not bear the test of God's word, yet souls will be deceived."[123]

---

*121 HTTP://ORDINATIONTRUTH.COM/WP-CONTENT/UPLOADS/2013/11/NAD-ORDINATION-14-MINORITY.PDF*

*122 HTTP://WWW.BIBLICA.COM/EN-US/BIBLE/BIBLE-FAQS/HOW-MANY-DIFFERENT-LANGUAGES-HAS-THE-BIBLE-BEEN-TRANSLATED-INTO/. ACCESSED MAY 10, 2014.*

*123 ELLEN G.WHITE, COUNSELS FOR THE CHURCH, P. 344.*

"With the cunning of the serpent they entrench themselves behind disconnected utterances construed to suit their carnal desires. Thus do many willfully pervert the word of God. Others, who have an active imagination, seize upon the figures and symbols of Holy Writ, interpret them to suit their fancy, with little regard to the testimony of Scripture as its own interpreter, and then they present their vagaries as the teachings of the Bible."[124]

Yet the servant of the Lord wrote the following in regards to the Scriptures: "The word and will of God are expressed in the Scriptures by inspired penmen. We should bind them as frontlets between our eyes, and walk according to their precepts; then we shall walk safely. Every chapter and every verse is a communication from God to man. In studying the word, the soul that hungers and thirsts for righteousness will be impressed by the divine utterances. Skepticism can have no power over a soul that with humility searches the Scriptures."[125] And concerning the final deception of Satan, she wrote: "Except those who are kept by the power of God, through faith in His word, the whole world will be swept into the ranks of this delusion."[126]

## WOMEN ELDERS IN THE NEW TESTAMENT?

When Christ chose His disciples, though there were many women who followed Him, He ordained only men. "And he ordained twelve, that they should be with him, and that he might send them forth to preach, And to have power to heal sicknesses, and to cast out devils: And Simon he surnamed Peter; And James the son of Zebedee, and John the brother of James; and he surnamed them Boanerges, which is, The sons of thunder: And Andrew, and Philip, and Bartholomew, and Matthew, and Thomas, and James the son of Alphaeus, and Thaddaeus, and Simon the Canaanite, And Judas Iscariot, which

---

124 *ELLEN G.WHITE, DARKNESS BEFORE DAWN, P. 7.*

125 *ELLEN G.WHITE, GOSPEL WORKERS, P. 140.*

126 *ELLEN G.WHITE, DARKNESS BEFORE DAWN, P. 23.*

also betrayed him: and they went into an house" (Mark 3:14-19). The argument is made that men were chosen because that was the culture of the times. Others suggest that the Bible is a chauvinistically slanted book. But to say or insinuate such is to cast a shadow upon God. The God of the New Testament is the same God of the Old Testament. It is Christ! While it is true that His chosen followers oftentimes buckled under and absorbed practices and ideas from the neighboring nations, He labored with them. By admonishing, chastening, and even allowing them to suffer the consequences of their cultural choices, He sought to guide them into a better way. And because He did not hide the waywardness of His people, the very evidence of His longsuffering and patience is used to negate His counsels.

Christ was not influenced by culture and He did not allow it to dictate His actions or words. He made decisions based on His wisdom and knowledge from His Father. He clearly stated, "My doctrine is not mine, but his that sent me. If any man will do his will, he shall know of the doctrine, whether it be of God, or whether I speak of myself" (John 7:16, 17). The Gospels themselves testify and thus contradict the conventional notions. It was because Christ was considered to be so antiestablishment to both the religious and civil government as well as to the culture and practice of His time that they could say, "Why eateth your Master with publicans and sinners? . . . Why do we and the Pharisees fast oft, but thy disciples fast not?" (Matthew 9:11-14) At another time they said, "Why do thy disciples transgress the tradition of the elders? for they wash not their hands when they eat bread" (Matthew 15:2). To all these futile charges to coerce Him to conform to the culture of the Jews, Jesus said, "Howbeit in vain do they worship me, teaching for doctrines the commandments of men. For laying aside the commandment of God, ye hold the tradition of men, as the washing of pots and cups: and many other such like things ye do" (Mark 7:7, 8).

When by craft they sought to prove Christ to be either an anarchist or a betrayer of the Jewish nation, they asked: "Is it lawful to give tribute to Caesar, or not? Shall we give, or shall we not give?" (Mark 12:14, 15). Jesus proved to be neither by stating, "Why tempt ye me? bring me a penny, that I may see it. And they brought it. And he saith unto them, Whose is this image and superscription? And they said unto him, Caesar's. And Jesus answering said unto them, Render to Caesar the things that are Caesar's, and to God the things that are God's" (verses 15-17).

The apostles were charged as being outlaws to civil authority. "These all do contrary to the decrees of Caesar, saying that there is another king, one Jesus" (Acts 17:7). The religious Jews charged that Paul "persuadeth men to worship God contrary to the law" (Acts 18:13). "And they are informed of thee, that thou teachest all the Jews which are among the Gentiles to forsake Moses, saying that they ought not to circumcise their children, neither to walk after the customs" (Acts 21:21). Neither culture nor customs of the times dictated the ministry of Christ or His disciples.

There is plenty of evidence that the women on His team were numerous. "And many women were there beholding afar off, which followed Jesus from Galilee, ministering unto him: Among which was Mary Magdalene, and Mary the mother of James and Joses, and the mother of Zebedee's children" (Matthew 27:55, 56).

Among these women was included His own mother. And if anybody would have been elevated with minimal resistance into a position in His church, it would have been the one whom God had chosen to borne Him of a virgin birth. Yet, when people attempted to place her in a privileged position, Jesus said, "Who is my mother? and who are my brethren? And he stretched forth his hand toward his disciples, and said, Behold my mother and my brethren!" (Matthew 12: 48, 49). Though Christ's tender regard for Mary as His mother was made quite obvious at the crucifixion, it is just as transparent that He did not lift her up above the men of His choosing.

The Bible also reveals that some of the women were persons of means and status. "There were also women looking on afar off: among whom was Mary Magdalene, and Mary the mother of James the less and of Joses, and Salome; (Who also, when he was in Galilee, followed him, and ministered unto him;) and many other women which came up with him unto Jerusalem." (Mark 15:40, 41). "And certain women, which had been healed of evil spirits and infirmities, Mary called Magdalene, out of whom went seven devils, And Joanna the wife of Chuza Herod's steward, and Susanna, and many others, which ministered unto him of their substance" (Luke 8:2, 3). Concerning this reference, The SDA Bible Commentary states: "One of the characteristics of the Gospel of Luke is its frequent references to Christ's ministry for the womenfolk of Palestine and the ministry of some of them on His behalf. This was something new, for the role of Jewish women in public life had been a relatively minor one, although in isolated instances, prophets like Elisha had ministered to women and been ministered to by them." In regards to Chuza, the Commentary further states, "Nothing further is known of this man. A steward held a position of no mean importance in the household he served (see on Matt. 20:8)." Joanna, "being the wife of Herod's steward, she must have been a person of wealth and influence."[127] Since she was a woman of high caliber and established financially, it would have been reasonable for Christ to have elevated her to the role of disciple. But Christ did not.

When it came to support Christ to go through the sacrifice, there were two humans sent. "And there appeared unto them Elias with Moses: and they were talking with Jesus" (Mark 9:4). It is a point to consider here that though there were women prophets in the Old Testament, such as Miriam (Exodus 15:20), Deborah (Judges 4:4), and Huldah (2 Kings 22:14), none are mentioned to have been elevated to the heights of these men, neither were women chosen to consult with him over the destiny of humanity.

Just as Christ began His earthly ministry by selecting men to take up the responsibility of the church, so He ended in the same manner. The fact that none of the other 70 disciples (Luke 10:1, 17) besides the 12 were mentioned as participating in the Last Supper, suggests a very important point. In Matthew 26:19 and 20 we read: "And the disciples did as Jesus had appointed them; and they made ready the passover. Now when the even was come, he sat down with the twelve." Here is an intentional exclusiveness. Christ permits none

---

127 *THE SDA BIBLE COMMENTARY, VOL. 5, PP. 769, 770.*

but the 12 to share the Last Supper with Him. Only 12 men partook of the sacred emblems. And it was to the 12 that Christ said, "Verily I say unto you, that ye which have followed me, in the regeneration when the Son of man shall sit in the throne of his glory, ye also shall sit upon twelve thrones, judging the twelve tribes of Israel" (Matthew 19:28).

According to the book of Hebrews, everything intended by the Savior to be implemented into the New Testament had to be put in place prior to His death. Paul wrote, "For where a testament is, there must also of necessity be the death of the testator. For a testament is of force after men are dead: otherwise it is of no strength at all while the testator liveth" (Hebrews 9:16, 17). Therefore, had Christ intended to place women in church leadership, He could have very well introduced them in this pivotal introduction of the New Testament. But He did not.

After the crucifixion weekend and the ascension of Christ, the believers gathered together in the upper room. "And when they were come in, they went up into an upper room, where abode both Peter, and James, and John, and Andrew, Philip, and Thomas, Bartholomew, and Matthew, James the son of Alphaeus, and Simon Zelotes, and Judas the brother of James. These all continued with one accord in prayer and supplication, with the women, and Mary the mother of Jesus, and with his brethren" (Acts 1:13, 14). During this convocation an important issue arose.

"Men and brethren, [Peter stated] this scripture must needs have been fulfilled, which the Holy Ghost by the mouth of David spake before concerning Judas, which was guide to them that took Jesus. For he was numbered with us, and had obtained part of this ministry. Now this man purchased a field with the reward of iniquity; and falling headlong, he burst asunder in the midst, and all his bowels gushed out. And it was known unto all the dwellers at Jerusalem; insomuch as that field is called in their proper tongue, Aceldama, that is to say, The field of blood. For it is written in the book of Psalms, Let his habitation be desolate, and let no man dwell therein: and his bishopric let another take. Wherefore of these men which have companied with us all the time that the Lord Jesus went in and out among us, Beginning from the baptism of John, unto that same day that he was taken up from us, must one be ordained to be a witness with us of his resurrection. And they appointed two, Joseph called Barsabas, who was surnamed Justus, and Matthias. And they prayed, and said, Thou, Lord, which knowest the hearts of all men, shew whether of these two thou hast chosen, That he may take part of this ministry and apostleship, from which Judas by transgression fell, that he might go to his own place. And they gave forth their lots; and the lot fell upon Matthias; and he was numbered with the eleven apostles" (verses 16-26).

No one can doubt that the Holy Spirit had taken charge of Peter and enlightened him concerning this important matter. Here was an opportunity for the New Testament church to be introduced to a new development. An apostolic position had just been recently vacated. Here was the perfect time to place one of the prominent women in this position. But though there were many devout women in the upper room, when it came to replacing the fallen disciple, the leaders were led by the Spirit to select another man. Please note that it was the Spirit's doing and not the apostles. The Spirit would not, and could not, have inserted a woman contrary to Jesus' final will and testament sealed with His blood.

In the fourth chapter of Revelation God reveals to John 24 thrones before the throne of God. "And round about the throne were four and twenty seats: and upon the seats I saw four and twenty elders sitting, clothed in white raiment; and they had on their heads crowns of gold" (Revelation 4:4). The Greek word from which "elder" has been translated is presbuteros.[128] It is used 72 times in the New Testament. In 57 instances it is used and translated into the English word "elder." The connotation is in reference to a man holding a position in the church, such as a pastor or other church leader. Ten times it is translated into "older man." This meaning assumes the quality of old age. Today we use the words "senior" or "elderly," meaning a person (man or woman) advanced in age, with the inference that wisdom

---

*128 STRONG'S CONCORDANCE, NO. 4245.*

comes with age. In other words they are leaders, in part, because of wisdom and spiritual maturity obtained through life.

Only once is the word translated into the English term "elder women" (1 Timothy 5:2). Paul was contrasting older men with older women, and younger men with younger women. In this particular situation, the apostle was simply making sure that the seniors are treated with respect, and that the younger are dealt with in purity.

Therefore, the evidence suggests that the 24 elders are men with a long experience with the Lord, and who are redeemed from the earth. The apostle Paul used the terms episkopos and presbuteros when referring to men in leadership. In Acts 20:17-35, as he was nearing the end of his ministry, he gave a final word of exhortation to the church in Ephesus. In verse 17 he addressed the presbuteros (elders) of the church. A few verses later, in verse 28, he referred to these same men as episkopos, or overseers. By describing the same group one time as presbuteros and a second time as episkopos, Paul seemed to consider the two words to be synonyms for men in the role of church leaders.

In Titus 1:5 Paul wrote to Titus to remind him that he left him in Crete with instructions to "ordain elders [presbuteros] in every city." To him an elder was clearly a position of leadership over a church. In verse 7 Paul began to describe the qualifications for an elder using the word episkopos (i.e., bishop) to describe this same group. Once again, Paul seemed to use these two words for men leaders interchangeably.

The motivation in all of this is to clarify that the word "elder" is masculine in nature and biblically speaking, a woman is never referenced as holding that title. Even during the days of Moses, when it was time to select people who would take part of Moses' burdens, the Lord directed the choice of burden bearers to be solely men. "The Lord directed Moses to gather before him seventy of the elders, whom he knew to be the elders of the people. They were not to be those only in advanced years, but men of dignity, sound judgment, and experience, who were qualified to be judges, or officers. 'And bring them unto the tabernacle of the congregation, that they may stand there with thee. And I will come down and talk with thee there; and I will take of the spirit which is upon thee, and will put it upon them, and they shall bear the burden of the people with thee, that thou bear it not thyself alone.'"[129]

In reading through Ellen White's writings, I have discovered the same use as found in the Bible. She uses the word "elder" exclusively for men. For example, she wrote, "It is quite possible that Elders Jones and Waggoner."130 In another place she wrote, "In company with Elders Whitney and Conradi."[131] When referring to the man and his spouse she wrote, "Elder and Mrs. Haskell were conducting Bible studies."[132]

## LEVELING THE PLAYING FIELD: GENDER EQUALITY

There is a text written by Paul that some present to suggest that in the New Testament dispensation Christ made no difference between male and female when it came to the ministry. The text cited is: "There is neither Jew nor Greek, there is neither bond nor free, there is neither male nor female: for ye are all one in Christ Jesus" (Galatians 3:28). But the preceding verse says, "For as many of you as have been baptized into Christ have put on Christ" (verse 27). This text makes plain the intention of the succeeding verse. It removes the human barriers set up by the Jews regarding acceptance by God based on distinction, caste, color, ethnicity, gender, or age.

Paul had already stated in verses 14-18: "That the blessing of Abraham might come on the Gentiles through Jesus Christ; that we might receive the promise of the Spirit through faith. . . . For if the

---

129 ELLEN G.WHITE, SPIRITUAL GIFTS, VOL. 4A, P. 16.

130 ELLEN G.WHITE, MANUSCRIPT RELEASES, VOL. 3, P. 201.

131 IBID., P. 393.

132 ELLEN G.WHITE, EVANGELISM, P. 470.

inheritance be of the law, it is no more of promise: but God gave it to Abraham by promise." And when writing to the Romans, he made it clear that "he is not a Jew, which is one outwardly; neither is that circumcision, which is outward in the flesh: But he is a Jew, which is one inwardly; and circumcision is that of the heart, in the spirit, and not in the letter; whose praise is not of men, but of God" (Romans 2:28, 29).

The apostle was following the teaching and practice of Christ. As a Jew, he was personally acquainted with the bigoted spirit cultivated against others. It was that spirit that arrogantly slandered Christ when they said, "Say we not well that thou art a Samaritan, and hast a devil?" (John 8:48). Calling Christ a Samaritan was intended as an insult, and calculated to distance the Jews from Him by raising their prejudices. That is why as a contrivance He told the good Samaritan story found in Luke 10:30-36. He also trained His disciples by calling the Syrophenician woman a dog (see Mark 7:26-28), and then telling her, "O woman, great is thy faith: be it unto thee even as thou wilt" (Matthew 15:28). And of the Roman centurion, He declared, "I have not found so great faith, no, not in Israel" (Matthew 8:10). By doing so, He sought to break down the walls between the races.

In his writings, the overwhelming burden of Paul is to help the Jews understand that salvation was not obtained by tracing their lineage or genealogy back to Abraham, but by faith in Christ, which was extended to any or all who would believe. There was a practice among Jews to trace their lineage back to Abraham, and place the fortunate person who could do so above all others. Jesus said to the Pharisees of His day, "And think not to say within yourselves, We have Abraham to our father: for I say unto you, that God is able of these stones to raise up children unto Abraham" (Matthew 3:9). To address this way of Jewish thinking, Paul wrote, "Neither give heed to fables and endless genealogies, which minister questions, rather than godly edifying which is in faith: so do" (1 Timothy 1:4). To Titus, he also wrote, "But avoid foolish questions, and genealogies, and contentions" (Titus 3:9).

No one in his or her right mind would take the passage of

Paul to its literal meaning. He was not saying that Christ erases gender or races. At the day of Pentecost Luke wrote that there were, "Parthians, and Medes, and Elamites, and the dwellers in Mesopotamia, and in Judaea, and Cappadocia, in Pontus, and Asia, Phrygia, and Pamphylia, in Egypt, and in the parts of Libya about Cyrene, and strangers of Rome, Jews and proselytes, Cretes and Arabians" (Acts 2:9-11). Paul wrote that there were Romans and Greeks, and, when traveling throughout Asia Minor, he refers to the Corinthians, Bereans, Philippians, Ephesians, and the Thessalonians, etc.

Women are still women, and men are still men. Women still give birth, while men do not. The equality suggested here is that of being eligible for salvation and heirs of the promises made to Abraham based on the exercise of faith on the part of anyone, whether they are male or female, adult or child, Jew or Gentile. Both men and women were equally expected to seek the Lord. The men's headship did not negate women's freedom, or even the expectation to have their own personal spiritual relationship with God independent of men. In the days of King Asa's rule he commanded: "Whosoever would not seek the Lord God of Israel should be put to death, whether small or great, whether man or woman" (2 Chronicles 15:13). They were also expected to own their responsibility when it came to taking care of their respective widows. Paul admonished: "If any man or woman that believeth have widows, let them relieve them, and let not the church be charged; that it may relieve them that are widows indeed" (1 Timothy 5:16). Just like the men, they could also equally contribute to God's cause. Moses wrote: "The children of Israel brought a willing offering unto the Lord, every man and woman, whose heart made them willing to bring for all manner of work, which the Lord had commanded to be made by the hand of Moses" (Exodus 35:29).

This equality issue has a way of muddying the waters. The words "equality" and "same" are not synonymous. Four U.S. quarters and one U.S. dollar bill are equal in value, but not the same in material or function. You can place four quarters in the coin slots of a washing machine to wash clothing, but a dollar bill will not work. Men and women are equal when it comes to salvation. The common denominator is the Lord. However, they are definitely not the same. This is true physically, emotionally, and even biologically. There are five factors that determine biological sex present at birth: the presence or absence of a Y chromosome, the type of gonads, the sex hormones, the internal reproductive anatomy (such as the uterus in women), and the external genitalia.[133] Paul's statement has not altered or eradicated this perpetual reality.

Biblically speaking, there have been occasions (besides Satan's attempt) that humans have made efforts to, quote, "level the playing field." Miriam's daring act of attempting to present herself as an equal with Moses, and the subsequent harsh rebuke with leprosy, stands as a warning to all. Miriam was not alone in her daring to presume herself to be equal with the chosen visible leader of Israel. The high priest Aaron, who happened to be her brother, unflinchingly stood in support of her. I suppose if she had not the support of the high priest she probably would never have had the courage to urge her rights of equality.

"In the affections of the people and the honor of Heaven she [Miriam] stood second only to Moses and Aaron. But the same evil that first brought discord in heaven sprang up in the heart of this woman of Israel, and she did not fail to find a sympathizer in her dissatisfaction. . . . Had Aaron stood up firmly for the right, he might have checked the evil; but instead of showing Miriam the sinfulness of her conduct, he sympathized with her, listened to her words of complaint, and thus came to share her jealousy." [134]

Miriam's and Aaron's jealousies were aroused by the appointment of the 70 elders without their consent. Neither of Moses' siblings was personally acquainted with the load and burden the Lord had placed upon him. To them it seemed that God had included them with equal authority; Moses was not to be the sole leader of Israel. After all, had not God chosen Aaron as the high priest, and she a

---

133 HTTP://EN.WIKIPEDIA.ORG/WIKI/SEX_DIFFERENCES_IN_HUMANS#CITE_NOTE-KNOXSCHACHT2011-1. KNOX, DAVID, PH.D., SCHACHT, CAROLINE, CHOICES IN RELATIONSHIPS: AN INTRODUCTION TO MARRIAGE AND THE FAMILY, 11 ED. (CENGAGE LEARNING, 2011) PP. 64-66, ACCESSED JUNE 17, 2013.

134 ELLEN G.WHITE, CONFLICT AND COURAGE, P. 104.

prophet? Why did Moses presume to consider himself as superior to them? These instigated feelings were reminiscent of the same motive that brought about the rebellion in heaven. In her frustrated aspiration she and Aaron demanded, "Hath the Lord indeed spoken only by Moses? hath he not spoken also by us?" (Numbers 12:2).

"And the Lord heard it. (Now the man Moses was very meek, above all the men which were upon the face of the earth.) And the Lord spake suddenly unto Moses, and unto Aaron, and unto Miriam, Come out ye three unto the tabernacle of the congregation" (verses 2-4). God was going to settle this sibling rivalry, and set the record straight.

"And the Lord came down in the pillar of the cloud, and stood in the door of the tabernacle, and called Aaron and Miriam: and they both came forth" (verse 5). Though Moses had been summoned, and appeared with his older sister and brother, the Lord did not address him. He is there only as a witness to observe what God was about to say and do. "And he said, Hear now my words: If there be a prophet among you, I the Lord will make myself known unto him in a vision, and will speak unto him in a dream. My servant Moses is not so, who is faithful in all mine house. With him will I speak mouth to mouth, even apparently, and not in dark speeches; and the similitude of the Lord shall he behold: wherefore then were ye not afraid to speak against my servant Moses?" (verses 6-8).

Consider what God is implying when He said to Miriam and Aaron that He speaks through dreams and visions to the prophets, but to Moses "mouth to mouth." In other words, I am the one who made Moses much higher than you as a prophet, Miriam. Where did you get this idea? It was not from Me speaking to you through a dream or vision, nor was it from My speaking to Moses. The implication is obvious. Her desire came from beneath, not from above.

In seeking to make herself equal with her younger brother, God considered Miriam guilty of being recalcitrant against not Moses, but God Himself. The swift retribution against her suggests in the strongest language that He considered her daring act of belligerence an affront against Himself for setting Moses above her. As much as she thought herself equal, God did not consider it so.

"And the cloud departed from off the tabernacle; and, behold, Miriam became leprous, white as snow: and Aaron looked upon Miriam, and, behold, she was leprous" (verse 10). The sin is so wicked that God's presence is withdrawn from the tabernacle. Clearly her desire for being treated equal in ministry was not a light matter with God. Nor is it today. The arch rebel instigated and filled her mind with a covetous spirit. But God will not subject Himself to comingle in a divided heart, nor share the same habitat with Satan.

"And Aaron said unto Moses, Alas, my lord, I beseech thee, lay not the sin upon us, wherein we have done foolishly, and wherein we have sinned. Let her not be as one dead, of whom the flesh is half consumed when he cometh out of his mother's womb. And Moses cried unto the Lord, saying, Heal her now, O God, I beseech thee. And the Lord said unto Moses, If her father had but spit in her face, should she not be ashamed seven days? let her be shut out from the camp seven days, and after that let her be received in again. And Miriam was shut out from the camp seven days: and the people journeyed not till Miriam was brought in again" (verses 11-15).

Miriam's sin is left recorded in a chapter completely dedicated to her aspiration of being equal based on her supposition that she was entitled to it. It is left for future generations of women as well as men who attempt to usurp or otherwise seek to push themselves into positions of equality not ordained of God. This heinous sin, spurred on by jealousy of this prophet and surmising that status qualified her to be on equal basis with God's elected leader, was immediately squelched. It was Aaron, the high priest, who was instrumental in supporting a woman to be elevated to the same level as the chosen spiritual leader of Israel. No doubt that his support emboldened her to pursue this equality. After all he was the high priest, a man of so great influence in all Israel that none but Moses stood above him. He had been elevated to that office by God himself, and should not his sister, a prophet, also share the ecclesiastical power?

What is amazing about this is that only Miriam was struck

with leprosy. Why not Aaron? One important reason is that he alone had been ordained to speak for Moses. God said to Moses, "Is not Aaron the Levite thy brother? I know that he can speak well. . . . And thou shalt speak unto him, and put words in his mouth: and I will be with thy mouth, and with his mouth, and will teach you what ye shall do. And he shall be thy spokesman unto the people: and he shall be, even he shall be to thee instead of a mouth, and thou shalt be to him instead of God" (Exodus 4:14-16). "And Moses and Aaron went and gathered together all the elders of the children of Israel: And Aaron spake all the words which the Lord had spoken unto Moses, and did the signs in the sight of the people" (verses 29, 30). Again in Exodus 7 God said to Moses, "See, I have made thee a god to Pharaoh: and Aaron thy brother shall be thy prophet. Thou shalt speak all that I command thee: and Aaron thy brother shall speak unto Pharaoh, that he send the children of Israel out of his land" (verses 1, 2).

In all of the negotiations with Egypt only Moses and Aaron were chosen to be God's representatives. Therefore, in this matter of who had the right to represent God, Aaron had been included, but not Miriam. Consequently, he was spared the scourge. She, the interloper, was not!

What a rebuke to Aaron. What feelings of consternation he must have felt realizing that it was his prodding and support that resulted in his sister being struck with a living death. In desperation he cried, no longer in tones of condescension, but in proper recognition of Moses' God-ordained authority: "Alas, my lord, I beseech thee, lay not the sin upon us, wherein we have done foolishly, and wherein we have sinned. Let her not be as one dead, of whom the flesh is half consumed when he cometh out of his mother's womb" (Numbers 12:11, 12). The realization of the magnitude of the offense constrained him to acknowledge their actions not as a mere error, nor as a justified beg for equality, but as it truly was - a sin.

God had lifted her up to the status of being a leader of the women. From the fact that the whole nation did not move until Miriam was permitted back into the camp, it is apparent that she was much loved and respected. But this was not enough. She wanted to lift herself up onto a higher level - an equality with Moses. But she was gravely mistaken.

Men and women have different roles and functions in life. A woman, as much as she may try, can never be a father. Conversely, a man can never be a mother. There are certain characteristics and qualities that a woman innately has that contribute to being a mother. On the other hand, men have certain characteristics that make him a father. In this sense, men and women are not equal - they were not made to be.

By instinct man is the provider, the protector; hence the title "husband" (Ruth 1:9; Ephesians 5:22-33; 1 Timothy 3:12). He is to be the house-band, the one who shields the family. He is the house builder who shelters his wife and children. By his inherent strength, man is capable of tasks generally never intended for a woman. He is the one who builds the dwelling, plows the fields, and hunts for food. God's instruction to the men was: "If he take him another wife; her food, her raiment, and her duty of marriage, shall he not diminish" (Exodus 21:10).

It is Christ Himself that established this headship. After the fall this ordained family structure was even more needful. Therefore, He declared: "Unto the woman he said, I will greatly multiply thy sorrow and thy conception; in sorrow thou shalt bring forth children; and thy desire shall be to thy husband, and he shall rule over thee. And unto Adam he said, Because thou hast hearkened unto the voice of thy wife, and hast eaten of the tree, of which I commanded thee, saying, Thou shalt not eat of it: cursed is the ground for thy sake; in sorrow shalt thou eat of it all the days of thy life" (Genesis 3:16, 17).

This was not just a temporary arrangement made by the Lord. The sorrow and pain in child birth has not ceased, nor will it until Revelation 21 is fulfilled, when God will then pronounce, "And I heard a great voice out of heaven saying, Behold, the tabernacle of God is with men, and he will dwell with them, and they shall be his people, and God himself shall be with them, and be their God. And God shall wipe away all tears from their eyes; and there shall be no more death, neither sorrow, nor crying, neither shall there be any more pain: for the former things are passed away" (Revelation 21:3, 4). It is not until this point, as ordained by the Lord, that the woman will have her sentence lifted, for she will no longer bear children (see Matthew 22:30; Mark 12:25; Luke 20:34-36), and the sorrow and pain will be no more. Therefore, it is until the fulfillment of this promise, that her "desire shall be to thy husband, and he shall rule over thee" (Genesis 3:16). This was a command of the Lord.

The sentence, "cursed is the ground for thy sake; in sorrow shalt thou eat of it all the days of thy life" (verse 17) was partially lifted after the Flood. God said, "I will not again curse the ground any more for man's sake; for the imagination of man's heart is evil from his youth; neither will I again smite any more every thing living, as I have done. While the earth remaineth, seedtime and harvest, and cold and heat, and summer and winter, and day and night shall not cease" (Genesis 8:21, 22).

The full removal will not be realized until the "new heavens and the new earth" (Isaiah 66:22; see also verse 23; Revelation 21:1, 2; 22:1, 2). "And they shall build houses, and inhabit them; and they shall plant vineyards, and eat the fruit of them. They shall not build, and another inhabit; they shall not plant, and another eat: for as the days of a tree are the days of my people, and mine elect shall long enjoy the work of their hands. They shall not labour in vain, nor bring forth for trouble; for they are the seed of the blessed of the Lord, and their offspring with them" (Isaiah 65:21-23).

Seth and his posterity, all the way through to Noah and his family, practiced this principle of man being the head of the family. This was the established order throughout the antediluvian times. The same was true with Noah's two faithful sons and their families. After them, during the patriarchal period, it is said of Abraham, "For I know him, that he will command his children and his household after him, and they shall keep the way of the Lord, to do justice and judgment; that the Lord may bring upon Abraham that which he hath spoken of him" (Genesis 18:19). This practice continued on throughout the entire Old Testament. The families of Isaac, Jacob, Joseph, David, and all those whose faith was in the living God followed the ordained chain of command that He ordered.

This domestic directive was inclusive and confirmed in the Ten Commandments. God said, "Remember the sabbath day, to keep it holy. Six days shalt thou labour, and do all thy work: But the seventh day is the sabbath of the Lord thy God: in it thou shalt not do any work, thou, nor thy son, nor thy daughter, thy manservant, nor thy maidservant, nor thy cattle, nor thy stranger that is within thy gates: For in six days the Lord made heaven and earth, the sea, and all that in them is, and rested the seventh day: wherefore the Lord blessed the sabbath day, and hallowed it" (Exodus 20:8-11).

While it is true that this commandment is inclusive of the wife, the language suggests that the man is responsible for ordering the home in Sabbath observance. This is illustrated in the lives of Noah, Abraham, Isaac, Jacob, etc. In the days of Nehemiah the Jewish men normally did the business transactions (see Nehemiah 13:15-22). And likewise, it was the "men of Tyre also therein, which brought fish, and all manner of ware, and sold on the sabbath unto the children of Judah, and in Jerusalem" (verse 16). Nehemiah held the men responsible for the transgression. He told them, "What evil thing is this that ye do, and profane the sabbath day? Did not your fathers thus, and did not our God bring all this evil upon us, and upon this city? yet ye bring more wrath upon Israel by profaning the Sabbath" (verses 17, 18). In this matter, the issue of equality was a moot issue. The Lord said, "Blessed is the man that doeth this, and the son of man that layeth hold on it; that keepeth the sabbath from polluting it, and keepeth his hand from doing any evil" (Isaiah 56:2).

The same is true in the tenth commandment. God said, "Thou shalt not covet thy neighbour's house, thou shalt not covet thy neighbour's wife, nor his manservant, nor his maidservant, nor his ox, nor his ass, nor any thing that is thy neighbour's" (Exodus 20:17). While it is true that this commandment appertained to both men and women as evidenced in the days of Christ (see John 8:3-11), the language is indicative that men are required to set the example. For a woman, in God's original creation, had no wife. However, this commandment also applies to women as evidenced by Eve's fall resulting from her desiring (ta'avah in Hebrew, see Genesis 3:6[135]), and also in the days of the apostles (see 2 Timothy 3:6).

There is one commandment that stands out when speaking about equality. When it came to honor and respect, both father and mother were to be equal recipients, for God said, "Honour thy father and thy mother: that thy days may be long upon the land which the Lord thy God giveth thee" (Exodus 20:12). This commandment, when considering intrinsic values, comes with promise of long life to anyone who regards the status of both mother and father as meriting respect on an equal basis. It is in these areas of intrinsic values that God levels the playing field. All should be honest, just, good, pure, holy, and devoted to God. In this area all should and can be equal. But when it comes to roles or positions in the church, all are not equal or the same.

As it was the case in biblical times, it is still the case today. Church elders have more authority than deacons (see Acts 6:2-7). They are equally sons of God (see Romans 8:14), but not equal in responsibilities before God (see 1 Timothy 5:17; James 5:14). Peter wrote: "The elders which are among you I exhort, who am also an elder, and a witness of the sufferings of Christ, and also a partaker of the glory that shall be revealed: Feed the flock of God which is among you, taking the oversight thereof, not by constraint, but willingly; not for filthy lucre, but of a ready mind; Neither as being lords over God's heritage, but being examples to the flock" (1 Peter 5:1-3).

The U.S. Declaration of Independence states: "All men are created equal . . . with certain unalienable Rights, that among these are Life, Liberty and the pursuit of Happiness." Nevertheless, all men are not equal when it comes to intelligence, strength, skills and abilities, endurance, and accomplishments. By nature they all have two legs and two arms. Yet, with two arms one is capable of building an empire. While another, also with two arms, accomplishes nothing more than extending the hand to beg for food. Equality is a relative term.

---

*135 STRONG'S LEXICON, NO. 8378.*

The beauty of God's creation is that He created us equal in the sense that both men and women are equally the children of God, but not equal in the sense that they are different from each other. He said, "Let us make man in our image, after our likeness: and let them have dominion over the fish of the sea, and over the fowl of the air, and over the cattle, and over all the earth, and over every creeping thing that creepeth upon the earth. So God created man in his own image, in the image of God created he him; male and female created he them" (Genesis 1:26, 27).

A statement by Ellen White affirms women's uniqueness: "Woman should fill the position which God originally designed for her, as her husband's equal. The world needs mothers who are mothers not merely in name, but in every sense of the word. We may safely say that the distinctive duties of woman are more sacred, more holy, than those of man. Let woman realize the sacredness of her work and in the strength and fear of God take up her life mission."[136] Just as Adam was to take his place as the father and husband of the home, Eve was to equally stand in her place as the mother and wife of her home. Here is the next paragraph: "The wife and mother should not sacrifice her strength and allow her powers to lie dormant, leaning wholly upon her husband. Her individuality cannot be merged in his. She should feel that she is her husband's equal—to stand by his side, she faithful at her post of duty and he at his.[137]

The diversity of man and woman was purposeful. Though symbiotic in creation, and designed to share equally in the bounties of all that God had made, they were not the same. God clearly placed man as the head of the household before the Fall. This was obvious by virtue of the fact that God formed the man first (see Genesis 2:7; 1 Timothy 2:13) and entrusted him with the dominion of the earth before God created the woman. The admonition to avoid the tree of knowledge of good and evil was given to Adam prior to Eve's creation (see Genesis 2:16, 17). This is apparently why God held Adam primarily responsible for the Fall (see Genesis 3:9-12, 16-24).

---

*136 ELLEN G.WHITE, THE ADVENTIST HOME, P. 231.*

*137 IBID.*

Then God provided a companion for Adam. He said, "It is not good that the man should be alone; I will make him an help meet for him" (Genesis 2:18). It was after that that from the man God made the woman (see verses 21-23). And when the first marriage was ordained, the language suggests that the man is the one to take the lead in leaving father and mother and cleaving to his wife, making the union of one flesh (see verse 24).

It should go without saying that since man was made in the likeness of God, Adam would naturally reflect and manifest the same love and care demonstrated to him by his Maker. Though created to be the leader, he would love his wife as "Christ . . . loved the church" (Ephesians 5:25). Being head did not translate into being a tyrant or slave driver, or being self-exalted or chauvinistic. On the contrary, angels, who excel in strength and who are made higher than man (see Psalm 8:5), are entrusted with the care of God's children (see Psalm 34:7; Hebrews 1:14). In opposition to the dialectic of determinism philosophy, the stronger beings are to use their superior powers not for the subjugation of others, but rather for their care and protection. Hence, the implication of Christ's words "For the poor always ye have with you" (John 12:8). To the self-exalting, self-serving, ambitious disciples He said, "If any man desire to be first, the same shall be last of all, and servant of all" (Mark 9:35). The principle of heaven is for the higher to help the lower, the smarter to use their intelligence for the benefit of those not so keen, the stronger to look out for the weaker, the one more capable to benefit the incapacitated. By nature, humans and animals are born helpless and totally dependent upon those capable of providing for their needs. In these situations equality is a moot issue.

Some use Jeremiah the prophet's words to suggest that God would change the order of a woman's relationship to man. Their supporting text says, "How long wilt thou go about, O thou backsliding daughter? for the Lord hath created a new thing in the earth, A woman shall compass a man" (Jeremiah 31:22). This prediction is couched in messianic language. A Jewish translation from the Hebrew reads, "How long will you hide, oh backsliding daughter? For the Lord has created a new thing [or novelty] on the earth, a woman [or female] shall encircle a man."[138] The Jewish commentary admits that "chapters 30 and 31 in the Book of Jeremiah are messianic texts with oracles of consolation for Israel."[139] The fulfillment of it was to occur after the 70-years prediction already given by the prophet concerning the return of the exiles back to Jerusalem. Jeremiah wrote, "And this whole land shall be a desolation, and an astonishment; and these nations shall serve the king of Babylon seventy years. And it shall come to pass, when seventy years are accomplished, that I will punish the king of Babylon, and that nation, saith the Lord, for their iniquity, and the land of the Chaldeans, and will make it perpetual desolations" (Jeremiah 25:11, 12).

Weddings were used as an indication of peaceful and prosperous conditions in a nation. In converse, the absences of weddings were used to describe the want, desolation, and adverse state of affairs of a nation. Jeremiah wrote: "Then will I cause to cease from the cities of Judah, and from the streets of Jerusalem, the voice of mirth, and the voice of gladness, the voice of the bridegroom, and the voice of the bride: for the land shall be desolate" (Jeremiah 7:34). This predicted condition was repeated several times in this prophet's writings (see Jeremiah 16:9; 25:10; 33:11). The psalmist wrote, "The fire consumed their young men; and their maidens were not given to marriage" (Psalm 78:63).

In the deliverance of His people from captivity God uses the bride and wedding imagery to symbolize the prosperous conditions returned back to them. He said through Isaiah, "Lift up thine eyes round about, and behold: all these gather themselves together, and come to thee. As I live, saith the Lord, thou shalt surely clothe thee with them all, as with an ornament, and bind them on thee, as a bride doeth. For thy waste and thy desolate places, and the land of thy destruction, shall even now be too narrow by reason of the inhabitants, and they that swallowed thee up shall be far away" (Isaiah 49:18,19).

---

*138 HTTP://THEJEWISHHOME.ORG/COUNTER/JER31_21.PDF.,WILL A BRIDE CIRCLE A GROOM, OR A DIVINE BABY FORM IN A VIRGIN'S WOMB? P. 3. ACCESSED APR. 24, 2014.*

*139 IBID.*

To attempt to take this verse and transport it, by virtue of a dual application of the prophecy, into our day would be out of sync. The prophet Joel wrote of our day, "Blow the trumpet in Zion, sanctify a fast, call a solemn assembly: Gather the people, sanctify the congregation, assemble the elders, gather the children, and those that suck the breasts: let the bridegroom go forth of his chamber, and the bride out of her closet. Let the priests, the ministers of the Lord, weep between the porch and the altar, and let them say, Spare thy people, O Lord, and give not thine heritage to reproach, that the heathen should rule over them: wherefore should they say among the people, Where is their God?" (Joel 2:15-17). Prior to the appearance of Christ's return to the earth at the Second Coming, the admonition, symbolically speaking, is to postpone any weddings and resort to weeping.

The complete overthrow and ultimate devastation predicted for mystical Babylon is portrayed by the absence of weddings. John wrote, "And the light of a candle shall shine no more at all in thee; and the voice of the bridegroom and of the bride shall be heard no more at all in thee: for thy merchants were the great men of the earth; for by thy sorceries were all nations deceived" (Revelation 18:23).

But in reference to God's people at the end of time, it is after the coming of Christ that the wedding feast takes place, and the bride encircles her Bridegroom, Christ. In fact, the final victory of Christ is pictured in marital language. Notice that the prophet John wrote: "Let us be glad and rejoice, and give honour to him: for the marriage of the Lamb is come, and his wife hath made herself ready. And to her was granted that she should be arrayed in fine linen, clean and white: for the fine linen is the righteousness of saints. And he saith unto me, Write, Blessed are they which are called unto the marriage supper of the Lamb" (Revelation 19:7-9). "And I John saw the holy city, New Jerusalem, coming down from God out of heaven, prepared as a bride adorned for her husband. . . . Come hither, I will shew thee the bride, the Lamb's wife. And he carried me away in the spirit to a great and high mountain, and shewed me that great city, the holy Jerusalem, descending out of heaven from God" (Revelation 21:2-10).

"The marriage relationship is often used in the Bible to represent the covenant relationship between God and His people (see Isa. 54:5; Jer. 3:14; Eze. 16:8-14; Hosea 2:19; 2 Cor. 11:2; Eph. 5:23, 27; Rev. 19:7; 21:2). As a bride brings joy to her husband, so the church brings joy to the heart of God. He will care for them as a faithful husband provides for and protects his beloved bride."[140]

In prophetic vision God reveals the final wedding to take place. It is after the saints have all been gathered to participate in the great marriage supper of the Lamb. Consequently, Jeremiah 31:22 either was fulfilled after the restoration of the Jews to the holy land in the days of Ezra and Nehemiah, or will be fulfilled after the second coming of Christ. In either scenario the encircling of the man by the woman is post deliverance, not pre. Therefore, seeing that the prophecy is messianic in nature, the application of "a woman shall compass a man" to mean that a woman becomes a pastor is incongruous. Making her a pastor does not level the playing field: it does the opposite. It places her in a role never intended for a female. It would be a new creation indeed—an oxymoron! It would be one that God never provided for in His Word, in His church, or in His inspirations to Ellen White.

## THE VOICE OF GOD

Christ had just left His disciples and went on His way to His Father (see Luke 24:51; Acts 1:9-11). These recently haggard men and women, battered by the trying events of the Passion Week, were left behind as His representatives. Christ charged, "All power is given unto me in heaven and in earth. Go ye therefore, and teach all nations, baptizing them in the name of the Father, and of the Son, and of the Holy Ghost: Teaching them to observe all things whatsoever I have commanded you: and, lo, I am with you alway, even unto the end of the world" (Matthew 28:18-20). "And that repentance and remission

---

*140 THE SDA BIBLE COMMENTARY, VOL. 4, P. 320.*

of sins should be preached in his name among all nations, beginning at Jerusalem. And ye are witnesses of these things" (Luke 24:47, 48). Prior to His departure, He organized them into a cohesive group called a church, and gave them their marching orders.

With this ecclesiastical authority they convened, and the first order of the church was to replace the fallen Judas (see Acts 1:13-20). In this convocation the Holy Spirit directed Peter to suggest the election of a successor. A qualification was required (verses 21, 22), and after the candidates were listed, the church voted, and Matthias was elected (verse 26). This election was regarded as the voice and will of God. "God has invested His church with special authority and power which no one can be justified in disregarding and despising, for he who does this despises the voice of God."[141]

"Christ gives power to the voice of the church. 'Verily I say unto you, Whatsoever ye shall bind on earth shall be bound in heaven: and whatsoever ye shall loose on earth shall be loosed in heaven.' No such thing is countenanced as one man's starting out upon his own individual responsibility and advocating what views he chooses, irrespective of the judgment of the church. God has bestowed the highest power under heaven upon His church. It is the voice of God in His united people in church capacity which is to be respected."[142]

The apostles held this understanding sacred. For example, when there was a division over what the Gentile believers could and could not practice as Christians, the church convened in Jerusalem. "And the apostles and elders came together for to consider of this matter" (Acts 15:6). After the discussion, "all the multitude kept silence" (verse 12). James, the chosen New Testament leader of the church, then gave the sentence. At the pronouncement made by the recognized leader (see Acts 21:18; 1 Corinthians 15:7; Galatians 2:9) those present were satisfied. "Then pleased it the apostles and elders with the whole church" (Acts 15:22). Once the vote was taken (the decision was made), the believers accepted it, and the record stated,

---

141 *ELLEN G.WHITE, THE ACTS OF THE APOSTLES, P. 163.*

142 *ELLEN G.WHITE, TESTIMONIES FOR THE CHURCH, VOL. 3, P. 450.*

"For it seemed good to the Holy Ghost, and to us, to lay upon you no greater burden than these necessary things" (verse 28). The church's decision was taken as the will, or voice, of God.

The principle of the "voice of God" speaking through the church was a well-established biblical concept and practice, which was understood and accepted in the Christian dispensation. It was also a principle held by the pioneers of the Adventist movement.

Prior to the Seventh-day Adventist Church being organized in 1863, the church was fragmented. The membership operated in a Congregational ecclesiastical system—what little there was of the church had varying organizations functioning independently of the other.

Since most Adventists came from institutionalized churches, and since most were well acquainted with the European history of the abuses, atrocities, persecutions, and hostilities by the institutional churches, they feared organization. Another fear was of the formalism that institutionalized denominations tended to degenerate into. They feared this formalism would make them part of "Babylon."

However, after the great disappointment of 1844, Adventist believers were loosely connected by a few common beliefs. They were:

1. *The second coming of Christ*
2. *The seventh-day Sabbath as the day of worship*
3. *The heavenly sanctuary and Christ's mediatory work*
4. *The gift of the Spirit of Prophecy.*

Though fear of organization existed among the believers, the growing numbers of the believers suggested that organization was inevitable. In 1850, a series of messages from Ellen G. White began to be circulated among the members that the believers must organize.

In 1901, Ellen White looked back at the experience and wrote:

"As our numbers increased, it was evident that without some form of organization there would be great confusion, and the work would not be carried forward successfully. To provide for the support of the ministry, for carrying the work in new fields, for protecting both the churches and the ministry from unworthy members, for holding church property, for the publication of the truth through the press, and for many other objects, organization was indispensable."[143]

During May 20-23, 1863, the delegates convened for a General Conference session. At that time there were 3,500 church members living in the Central and New England States. It was at this gathering that a General Conference president was elected. His name was John Byington. He became the first General Conference president. His tenure was from May 20, 1863, to May 17, 1865. At this meeting a General Conference committee was elected. It was made up of:

1. *John Byington*
2. *J. N. Andrews*
3. *G.W. Amadon*

The decision proved to be blessed by the Lord, for the work grew rapidly. But as the work grew, problems developed. By this time there were several independent organizations. There were the following:

a. *International Medical Missionary and Benevolent Association*
b. *International Sabbath School Association*
c. *International Tract Society*
d. *National Religious Liberty Association*
e. *Foreign Mission Board*

Though they were operated by Seventh-day Adventists, they were all independent of the General Conference. Another formidable

---

143 ELLEN G. WHITE, TESTIMONIES TO MINISTERS AND GOSPEL WORKERS, P. 26.

challenge was the burgeoning medical work established in Battle Creek, Michigan. Its leader was a bright young fledging physician named J. Harvey Kellogg. He had a strong medical program that was becoming renowned throughout the nation and abroad. He developed a missionary organization—which sent out its own missionaries. These agencies had no connection with the church. In fact, he tried to bring other health institutions under his control. By 1901 he had 2,000 people on payroll, while the church had 1,500 in all lines of work.

In October of 1888, there was another General Conference session. During those meetings Elder O. A. Olsen was elected president. It was also at this gathering that Jones and Waggoner presented messages on righteousness by faith. A number of leading men rose up against Jones and Waggoner. And because Ellen White supported Jones and Waggoner on this point, the others opposed her and managed to get her a call to Australia.[144]

Gradually some of these accepted the message of righteousness by faith and put their support behind Ellen White. However, some did not. Two or three of these men were accepted by President Olsen as his key advisors. Those who were elected and became aides to the new General Conference president and served from 1888 to 1901 were:

*A. A. R. Henry*

1. *General Conference treasurer 1883-1888.*
2. *From 1882 to 1897 involved with treasury of SDA Publishing Association at Battle Creek.*
3. *Between 1893 and 1895 he was both treasurer and manager.*
4. *Simultaneously he was a member of nearly all early SDA medical and educational institutions in the Central and Western States.*

*B. Harmon Lindsay*

1. *Treasurer of General Conference from 1874 to 1875 and 1888 to 1893.*

---

*144 ELLEN G.WHITE, MANUSCRIPT RELEASES,VOL. 2, P. 150.*

2. *Participated in establishment of Battle Creek and Oakwood colleges.*

3. *Served as treasurer of several institutions.*
4. *Among them Review and Herald in the 1890s.*
5. *Left Adventist Church and became Christian Scientist.*

C. *Clement Eldridge*

1. *Publishing and religious liberty leader.*
2. *In 1887 his name appeared as auditor of Review and Herald.*
3. *1889-1892 or 1893, general manager of Review and Herald.*
4. *Joined a private publishing firm in Chicago.*

These men, and others under their influence, worked contrary to God's purposes and counsels given by Ellen White, and swept President O. A. Olsen along with them. She wrote: "Elder Olsen's advisers were blinding his eyes so that he should see through the eyes of these men who were preaching under a deception."[145]

Problems began to be manifested in several ways. They had no intention of carrying out what was voted by the boards.[146] To this concern, she wrote: "But men, human men, have had a settled determination to carry out their own devisings as if the Lord had authorized them to do this work. Men were working upon principles that God has condemned, which God will not accept, but in the great day of God He will say, 'Who has required this work at your hands?'"[147]

In spite of the counsel, Elder Olsen would send for them to advise and counsel him when they were not consecrated to God. Again, addressing the problem, she wrote: "It has been a mystery to me how Elder Olsen could receive and sanction two men [A. R. Henry and Harmon Lindsay] of similar religious character, when he has no evidence that they are consecrated to God."[148] "The Lord has a

---

145 *ELLEN G.WHITE MANUSCRIPT 33, 1891.*

146 *IBID.*

147 *ELLEN G.WHITE MANUSCRIPT 57, 1895*

148 *ELLEN G.WHITE, MANUSCRIPT RELEASES,VOL. 17, P. 171.*

controversy with them, and yet Elder Olsen treats them as representative men, sending them hither and thither as men of discernment, endorsing them as trustworthy and reliable men, to whom the people shall listen and show respect as the voice of God in the conference."[149]

To describe what was taking place, she coined the words "kingly power." This was a term used by Ellen White in describing the dealings of these men and what motivated them.

"Over and over again men have said 'The voice of the conference is the voice of God; therefore everything must be referred to the conference. The conference must permit or restrict in the various lines of work.' As the matter has been presented to me, there is a narrow compass, and within this narrow compass all the entrances to which are locked, are those who would like to exercise kingly power. But the work carried on all over the field demands an entirely different course of action."[150]

"Everything that has been planned in regard to consolidation shows that men are seeking to grasp the scepter of power and hold control over human minds. But God does not work with them in their devising, and the voice they now have in the cause of God is not the voice of God. They have proved themselves utterly unworthy of a place as wise managers; for their strength is used to turn men away from their rights to benefit themselves."[151]

It was during this time that the Review and Herald Publishing Association was cheating authors, including Uriah Smith, out of royalties. All decisions for the whole work were being made by these few men, even though the General Conference Committee by 1901, was made up of 13 men. While still in Australia, Ellen White was receiving insights from God concerning these men. She wrote: "Men have seemed determined to place the mold and superscription of their human wisdom upon the work of God. They refused to be worked by

149 IBID., P. 172.

150 ELLEN G.WHITE MANUSCRIPT 43, 1901, PP. 1, 2.

151 ELLEN G.WHITE, TESTIMONIES TO MINISTERS AND GOSPEL WORKERS, P. 291

the Holy Spirit, and brought in their own wisdom and devising. The result of this has been seen in various ways. The sacred character of the cause of God is no longer realized at the center of the work. The voice from Battle Creek, which has been regarded as authority in counseling how the work should be done, is no longer the voice of God; but it is the voice of - whom?"[152]

"You have thought that whatever your councils decided, would stand as the voice of God; but this supposition must no longer exist. You have the Word of God; you have the message which God has given; but you have turned away from obeying this Word."[153]

During this period Ellen White speaks of the voice of the General Conference as no longer being the voice of God. And, for good reason, she wrote: "This is the reason I was obliged to take the position that there was not the voice of God in the General Conference management and decisions. Methods and plans would be devised that God did not sanction, and yet Elder Olsen made it appear that the decisions of the General Conference were as the voice of God. Many of the positions taken, going forth as the voice of the General Conference, have been the voice of one, two, or three men who were misleading the Conference." [154]

In spite of all that was taken place under President Olson's leadership, Ellen White's heart went out to Elder Olsen, yet she did not excuse him for his mistakes. "I have the tenderest sympathy for your president, Elder Olsen. I know his soul is weighed down with burdens; and unless those connected with him have the Holy Spirit's guidance, mistakes of a serious character will be made."[155] (This letter was sent to the 1895 General Conference session.)

---

*152 ELLEN G.WHITE, THE ELLEN G.WHITE 1888 MATERIALS (1987), P. 1582.*

*153 ELLEN G.WHITE, MANUSCRIPT RELEASES, VOL. 17, P. 196.*

*154 IBID., P. 166.*

*155 IBID., P. 171.*

What resulted from the apparent chaotic state of the church was that some men arose and began calling the church "Babylon." The men's names were Stanton and Caldwell. They published some tracts calling the church "Babylon." In it they stated:

1. *The Loud Cry! Babylon Fallen!*
2. *Say SDA Church is Babylon.*
3. *Loud cry of Rev., "come out of them, My people," is a call out of the SDA church.*

Ellen White's replies were later published in an article in the Review and Herald (Nov. 8, 1956). She wrote: "These people are not Babylon; for Thou hast given to them righteousness and peace and thy joy, that their joy may be full."[156]

"How could they [Stanton] come from that meeting where the power of God was revealed in so marked a manner, and proclaim that the loud cry was that the commandment-keeping people were Babylon?[157]

"I have no such message to give; but one of an entirely different character."[158]

"Beware of those who arise with a great burden to denounce the church. The chosen ones who are standing and breasting the storm of opposition from the world, and are uplifting the downtrodden commandments of God to exalt them as honorable and holy, are indeed the light of the world."[159]

"How dare mortal man pass his judgment upon them, and call the church a harlot, Babylon, a den of thieves. . . ."[160]

"When anyone is drawing apart from the organized body of

156 ELLEN G. WHITE, QUOTED IN REVIEW AND HERALD, NOVEMBER 8, 1956.

157 IBID.

158 IBID.

159 IBID.

160 ELLEN G. WHITE, THIS DAY WITH GOD, P. 172.

God's commandment-keeping people, when he begins to weigh the church in his human scales and begins to pronounce judgment against them, then you may know that God is not leading him. He is on the wrong track."[161]

More can be read about the church not being "Babylon" in Testimonies to Ministers and Gospel Workers, in the chapter "The Remnant Church Not Babylon."

In all of this there were some interesting dynamics:

1. *God reproved His church.*
2. *They were still His people, despite their problems.*
3. *God worked His will by protecting the church and resolving the problems.*

Finally, in the General Conference session that convened in 1901, some major changes came:

1. *Complete reorganization that corrected the weaknesses of previous administrations."That these men should stand in a sacred place, to be as the voice of God to the people, as we once believed the General Conference to be, - that is past. What we want now is a reorganization. We want to begin at the foundation, and to build upon a different principle."*[162]

2. *Steps were taken for reorganization.*
a. *Enlarge General Conference Committee.*
b. *Bring all separate independent entities together under leadership of General Conference.*
c. *Form departments within the General Conference that supervised these activities.*
d. *Set up union conferences.*
e. *Local and union conferences were given the responsibilities of the daily work of various fields.*

To these reorganizational changes Ellen White exultingly rejoiced and wrote: "During the General Conference the Lord wrought

---

161 *ELLEN G.WHITE, LAST DAY EVENTS, P. 51.*

162 *ELLEN G.WHITE, IN GENERAL CONFERENCE BULLETIN, APR. 3, 1901.*

mightily for His people. Every time I think of that meeting, a sweet solemnity comes over me, and sends a glow of gratitude to my soul. We have seen the stately steppings of the Lord our Redeemer. We praise His holy name; for He has brought deliverance to His people."163

Although the chaos was brought under control and the wrongs were corrected, Edson White, Ellen White's son, was still smarting from unjust dealings with the Review and Herald board and quoted words his mother penned prior to 1901 (letter 54, 1901). Upon discovering what he was doing, she again took to her pen and wrote: "I am again much burdened as I see you selecting words from writings that I have sent you, and using them to force decisions that the brethren do not regard with clearness."164

"Your course would have been the course to be pursued if no change had been made in the General Conference. But a change has been made, and many more changes will be made and great developments will be seen."165

"It hurts me to think that you are using words which I wrote prior to the Conference. Since the Conference great changes have been made."166

"A terribly unjust course has been pursued in the past. A want of principle has been revealed. But in pity to His people God has brought about changes."167

"The course of action which before the conference might have been a necessity, is no longer a necessity; for the Lord Himself interposed to set things in order. He has given His Holy Spirit. I am confident that He will set in order the matters that seem to be movin

---

163 *ELLEN G.WHITE, IN REVIEW AND HERALD, NOV. 26, 1901.*

164 *ELLEN G.WHITE, MANUSCRIPT RELEASES,VOL. 19, P. 146.*

165 *IBID.*

166 *IBID.,VOL. 3, P. 205.*

167 *IBID.*

wrong."[168]

Several years later Ellen White was still satisfied that that Lord had stabilized His church, and as a result she repeatedly assured the people of God's love and guidance.

"We cannot now step off the foundation that God has established. We cannot now enter into any new organization, for this would mean apostasy from the truth."[169]

In a final effort to set the record straight, Ellen White was led to reaffirm the position of the church in relationship to being reinstated as it stood prior to the period that she called "kingly power." She wrote: "I have often been instructed by the Lord that no man's judgment should be surrendered to the judgment of any other one man. Never should the mind of one man or the minds of a few men be regarded as sufficient in wisdom and power to control the work and to say what plans shall be followed. But when, in a General Conference, the judgment of the brethren assembled from all parts of the field is exercised, private independence and private judgment must not be stubbornly maintained, but surrendered. Never should a laborer regard as a virtue the persistent maintenance of his position of independence, contrary to the decision of the general body."[170]

"At times, when a small group of men entrusted with the general management of the work have, in the name of the General Conference, sought to carry out unwise plans and to restrict God's work, I have said that I could no longer regard the voice of the General Conference, represented by these few men, as the voice of God. But this is not saying that the decisions of a General Conference composed of an assembly of duly appointed, representative men from all parts of the field should not be respected. God has ordained that the representatives of His church from all parts of the earth, when assembled in a General Conference, shall have authority. The error that some are

---

*168 IBID.*

*169 ELLEN G.WHITE, CHRIST TRIUMPHANT, P. 367.*

*170 ELLEN G.WHITE, TESTIMONIES FOR THE CHURCH, VOL. 9, P. 260.*

in danger of committing is in giving to the mind and judgment of one man, or of a small group of men, the full measure of authority and influence that God has vested in His church in the judgment and voice of the General Conference assembled to plan for the prosperity and advancement of His work."[171]

"God has invested His church with special authority and power which no one can be justified in disregarding and despising, for he who does this despises the voice of God."[172]

"I am encouraged and blessed as I realize that the God of Israel is still guiding His people and that He will continue to be with them, even to the end."[173] (From Ellen White's final message to the Seventh-day Adventist Church in General Conference session. These reassuring words were read to the session by the General Conference president, A. G. Daniells, on May 27, 1913.)

There have been two separate General Conference sessions - Indianapolis, Indiana, in 1990, and Utrecht, Netherlands, in 1995 - in which the issue of ordaining women was presented to its delegates. After much discussion, the delegates voted to deny the request of the North American Division to ordain women as pastors.

Prior to the 2010 General Conference session, the former General Conference president decided to test the waters prior to resubmitting another request to the world body for reconsideration of the issue. The 13 General Conference division leaders were requested to consider the matter at their respective division constituency meetings. I was among the delegates that discussed the issue at the Southern Asia-Pacific Division, headquartered in Cavite, Philippines. Our division president had asked a scholar to present a talk to the delegates on the Adventist historical perspective of ordination. Instead, he presented a talk on why women should be ordained.

---

*171 IBID.*

*172 ELLEN G.WHITE, THE ACTS OF THE APOSTLES, P. 164.*

*173 ELLEN G.WHITE, SELECTED MESSAGES, VOL. 2, P. 406.*

At the conclusion of his presentation I went to the microphone and asked, "Mr. Chairman, we have heard a presentation on why women should be ordained. Did you ask someone to present the opposite view on why women should not be ordained? That way, the delegates can have the prerogative of both views to consider."

He simply said, "No. I asked him to present the Adventist historical perspective on ordination."

I then asked, "Do you have someone ready to present the opposite view?"

His answer was "No."

The meeting was then adjourned, and all vacated the meeting room. I left troubled by the proceedings. That night I awakened around 3:00 a.m. with my mind filled with verses and information. Realizing the import of what was happening, I quickly got up and started writing as fast as I could, fearing that I would lose the thoughts if I delayed. By 7:00 a.m. I had several pages filled with the thoughts that filled my mind. I then e-mailed the division president the information that had been presented to me. At 8:00 a.m. the meeting was about to reconvene. I rushed to the president and asked if he had read the materials I had sent him. "No," he said. "Let me go to my office." When he returned, he had already had his secretary print enough copies for all the delegates.

After the devotional, he made mention that subsequent to the inquiry concerning the former day's issue on women's ordination, Mr. Torres would present the opposite view. Frankly, I was surprised. I thought that by sending the information to him he would be more informed concerning the biblical perspective on ordination. Since I was on the spot, I did get up and make my presentation. I began with the last two concluding statements of the presenter who had been in favor of women pastors. The first: "By the way, you should know that Ellen White had ministerial credentials." Second, "Phebe of the Bible was a deacon." To the first, I said, "It is true that Mrs. White had ministerial credentials; however, she never allowed herself to be ordained.

Second, "Phebe was a deaconess; the Greek word for 'servant' is in the feminine." "Point well taken," responded the former speaker.

After my presentation, a debate ensued. After which, the chairman called for a vote on the issue. It was voted down by more than 75 percent of those present. It was interesting to note that the greater number of women present voted against the issue.

When the division leaders reconvened at the General Conference and gave their reports, it was discovered that the delegates of 9 of the 13 divisions voted against the proposed issue. Consequently, the topic was not presented to the 4,000 delegates that met in Atlanta, Georgia, for the 2010 General Conference session.

Contrary to the decisions taken in those General Conference sessions, two unions acted independently and ordained some women. These actions created a situation that the world church was forced to address. In the Annual Council of 2013 the delegates representing the world church took the following action:

"Decisions to pursue a course of action not in harmony with the 1990 and 1995 General Conference session decisions (with respect to ministerial ordination) represent not only an expression of dissent but also a demonstration of self-determination in a matter previously decided by the collective church," the statement said. "The General Conference Executive Committee regards these actions as serious mistakes."[174]

These actions on the part of these unions raised serious concerns on the part of many who believe that when the General Conference meets in session and votes an action it is considered as the voice of God. Those in North America have taken the liberty to annul the General Conference decisions, and, contrary to its vote, have ordained women. The question then remains, does the vote of a world-

---

*174 HTTP://WWW.COLUMBIAUNION.ORG/ARTICLE/1383/SERVICES/ADMINISTRATION/OFFICE-OF-THE-PRESIDENT/2012-SPECIAL-CONSTITUENCY/OCTOBER-16-2012-STATEMENT-ON-CHURCH-POLITY-PROCEDURES-AND-RESOLUTION-OF-DISAGREEMENTS-IN-THE-LIGHT-OF-RECENT-UNION-ACTIONS-ON-MINISTERIAL-ORDINATION. ACCESSED JULY 20, 2014.*

wide church dully called for meeting still stand as the voice of God? The historical evidence confirms that it does!

## HANDS-ON WOMEN

In looking up Ellen G. White's statements on ordination, I found 93 results using that specific word or term. To determine its use, consideration was given to each one as used in context. What I have discovered is that each time she used the term, she used it in association with men being called, or ordained. Not once was there found a reference in her writings that included a woman being called to be an ordained minister. There are 1049 references using the word "ordained." The majority of the time, the word is used with the sense of "establishing," "mandating," etc. None that I have read that referred to a call to be a pastor ever mentions a woman.

When it comes to being ordained to the gospel ministry, Ellen White is very clear as to what gender. In The Acts of the Apostles she wrote, "Since His ascension Christ has carried forward His work on the earth by chosen ambassadors, through whom He speaks to the children of men and ministers to their needs. The great Head of the church superintends His work through the instrumentality of men ordained by God to act as His representatives."[175]

"The position of those who have been called of God to labor in word and doctrine for the upbuilding of His church, is one of grave responsibility. In Christ's stead they are to beseech men and women to be reconciled to God, and they can fulfill their mission only as they receive wisdom and power from above.[176]

There are statements referring to women having hands laid on as deacons and gospel workers, but never as pastors. There are statements that speak of people who can work for the Lord without

---

*175 ELLEN G. WHITE, THE ACTS OF THE APOSTLES, P. 360.*

*176 IBID.*

having hands laid on them in ordination. Those statements are included below.

Therefore, the more I study the subject and consider the attitude of some, the more convinced I am that ordination is presently being treated as nothing more than a mere title, rather than a sacred calling for men to enter full-time ministry.

"For many years Ellen White was voted ministerial credentials by the Michigan Conference (See E. G. White, Review and Herald, September 10, 1872) and then later by the General Conference. However, she was never ordained by human hands, nor did she ever perform a wedding, organize a church, or conduct a baptism."[177]

Women should have had hands laid on them to do deacon type of work. They were ordained as deacons, but never elders or pastors in Ellen White's time. Notice the statements below:

"A number of women were ordained as deaconesses during Ellen White's Australian ministry. On August 10, 1895, the nominating committee at the Ashfield church in Sydney rendered its report, which was approved. The clerk's minutes for that date state: 'Immediately following the election, the officers were called to the front where pastors Corliss and McCullagh set apart the elder, deacons, [and] deaconesses by prayer and the laying on of hands.'"[178]

"Several years later, in the same church, W. C. White officiated at the ordination of the church officers. The minutes of the Ashfield church for January 7, 1900, state: 'The previous Sabbath officers had been nominated and accepted for the current year, and today Elder White ordained and laid hands on the Elders, Deacon, and Deaconesses.' AR, January 16, 1986."[179]

---

177 *ELLEN G.WHITE, DAUGHTERS OF GOD, P. 248.*

178 *IBID.*

179 *IBID.*

Just as in New Testament times, when the rank and file of the believers "went every where preaching the word" (Acts 8:4) without being ordained, so people today can work without being ordained. Notice the following statements:

"While some with special talents are chosen to devote all their energies to the work of teaching and preaching the gospel, many others, upon whom human hands have never been laid in ordination, are called to act an important part in soulsaving. . . . The self-sacrificing servant of God who labors untiringly in word and doctrine, carries on his heart a heavy burden. . . . His wages do not influence him in his labor. . . . From heaven he received his commission, and to heaven he looks for his recompense when the work entrusted to him is done."[180]

"Aquila and Priscilla were not called to give their whole time to the ministry of the gospel, yet these humble laborers were used by God to show Apollos the way of truth more perfectly. The Lord employs various instrumentalities for the accomplishment of His purpose, and while some with special talents are chosen to devote all their energies to the work of teaching and preaching the gospel, many others, upon whom human hands have never been laid in ordination, are called to act an important part in soulsaving."[181]

Ellen White refers to men only as candidates for the ordained ministry or eldership:

1. *"God has repeatedly shown that persons should not be encouraged into the field without unmistakable evidence that He has called them. The Lord will not entrust the burden for his flock to unqualified individuals. Those whom God calls must be men of deep experience, tried and proved, men of sound judgment, men who will dare to reprove sin in the spirit of meekness, men who understand how to feed the flock. God knows the heart, and He knows whom to select."*[182]

---

180 *ELLEN G.WHITE, CONFLICT AND COURAGE, P. 342.*

181 *ELLEN G.WHITE, THE ACTS OF THE APOSTLES, P. 355.*

182 *ELLEN G.WHITE, TESTIMONIES FOR THE CHURCH, VOL. 1, P. 209.*

2. *"After these have had some experience, there is still another work to be done for them. They should be presented before the Lord in earnest prayer that He would indicate by His Holy Spirit if they are acceptable to Him. The apostle says: 'Lay hands suddenly on no man.' In the days of the apostles the ministers of God did not dare to rely upon their own judgment in selecting or accepting men to take the solemn and sacred position of mouthpiece for God. They selected the men whom their judgment would accept, and then they placed them before the Lord to see if He would accept them to go forth as His representatives. No less than this should be done now."*[183]

3. *"In many places we meet men who have been hurried into responsible positions as elders of the church when they are not qualified for such a position. They have not proper government over themselves. Their influence is not good. The church is in trouble continually in consequence of the defective character of the leader. Hands have been laid too suddenly upon these men."*[184]

4. *"Ministers of God should be of good repute, capable of discreetly managing an interest after they have aroused it. We stand in great need of competent men who will bring honor instead of disgrace upon the cause which they represent. Ministers should be examined especially to see if they have an intelligent understanding of the truth for this time, so that they can give a connected discourse upon the prophecies or upon practical subjects. If they cannot clearly present Bible subjects they need to be hearers and learners still. They should earnestly and prayerfully search the Scriptures, and become conversant with them, in order to be teachers of Bible truth to others. All these things should be carefully and prayerfully considered before men are hurried into the field of labor."*[185]

5. *"No man should be set apart as a teacher of the people while his own teaching or example contradicts the testimony God has given His servants to bear in regard to diet, for this will bring confusion. His disregard of health reform unfits him to stand as the Lord's messenger."*[186]

The term or title "elder" is a masculine title and biblically speaking, never applied to women.

The title "elders" is found 179 times in the entire Bible. None of them ever refers to a woman. (See Strong's Exhaustive Lexicon.)

---

183 IBID., VOL. 4, P. 406. (ITALICS SUPPLIED.)

184 IBID. (ITALICS SUPPLIED.)

185 IBID., P. 407. (ITALICS SUPPLIED.)

186 IBID., VOL. 6, P. 378. (ITALICS SUPPLIED.)

*1. Concerning the Jerusalem Council, which convened to determine the "Gentile" issue; Ellen White wrote: "The entire body of Christians was not called to vote upon the question. The 'apostles and elders,' men of influence and judgment, framed and issued the decree, which was thereupon generally accepted by the Christian churches. Not all, however, were pleased with the decision; there was a faction of ambitious and self-confident brethren who disagreed with it. These men assumed to engage in the work on their own responsibility. They indulged in much murmuring and faultfinding, proposing new plans and seeking to pull down the work of the men whom God had ordained to teach the gospel message. From the first the church has had such obstacles to meet and ever will have till the close of time."*[187]

*2. "Since His ascension Christ has carried forward His work on the earth by chosen ambassadors, through whom He speaks to the children of men and ministers to their needs. The great Head of the church superintends His work through the instrumentality of men ordained by God to act as His representatives."*[188]

*3. "Pastors are needed—faithful shepherds—who will not flatter God's people, nor treat them harshly, but who will feed them with the bread of life—men who in their lives feel daily the converting power of the Holy Spirit and who cherish a strong, unselfish love toward those for whom they labor."*[189]

*4. "Peter here used a figure of speech familiar to the priests. The prophets had spoken of the rejected stone; and Christ Himself, speaking on one occasion to the priests and elders, said: 'Did ye never read in the Scriptures, The stone which the builders rejected, the same is become the head of the corner: this is the Lord's doing, and it is marvelous in our eyes? Therefore say I unto you, The kingdom of God shall be taken from you, and given to a nation bringing forth the fruits thereof. And whosoever shall fall on this stone shall be broken: but on whomsoever it shall fall, it will grind him to powder' (Matthew 21:42-44)."*[190]

---

187 ELLEN G. WHITE, THE ACTS OF THE APOSTLES, P. 196. (ITALICS SUPPLIED.)

188 IBID., P. 360. (ITALICS SUPPLIED.)

189 IBID., P. 526.

190 IBID., P. 64.

# WORKERS NOT ORDAINED, STILL RECOGNIZED BY HEAVEN

There are two words or terms that can be confusing when broaching the topic of ordination. They are "ministry" and "minister." Ministry is a task, while minister is a role or position. The first can be done by anyone who is a believer. The second is a position consigned to those called to serve in a pastor's role. Biblically speaking, as already clarified, it is the role of an overseer called "elder" or "bishop."

For the purpose of doing ministry there need not be any hand placed on man or woman. This work is incumbent on all to carry on once they have pledged their allegiance to Christ in baptism. Consider the following quotes:

1. *"Have you tasted of the powers of the world to come? Have you been eating the flesh and drinking the blood of the Son of God? Then, although ministerial hands may not have been laid upon you in ordination, Christ has laid His hands upon you and has said: 'Ye are My witnesses.'"*[191]

2. *"There are many who are laborers together with God whom we do not discern. The hands of ministers have never been laid upon them in ordination for the work; but nevertheless they are wearing the yoke of Christ, and exert a saving influence in working in different lines to win souls to Christ. The success of our work depends upon our love to God and our love to our fellowmen. When there is harmonious action among the individual members of the church, when there is love and confidence manifested by brother to brother, there will be proportionate force and power in our work for the salvation of men. Oh, how greatly we need a moral renovation! Without the faith that works by love, you can do nothing. May the Lord give you hearts to receive this testimony."*[192]

3. *"Aquila and Priscilla were not called to give their whole time to the ministry of the gospel, yet these humble laborers were used by God to show Apollos the way of truth more perfectly. The Lord employs various instrumentalities for the accomplishment of His purpose; and while some with special talents are chosen to devote all their energies to the work of teaching and preaching the gospel, many others, upon whom human hands have never been*

---

191 ELLEN G. WHITE, TESTIMONIES FOR THE CHURCH, VOL. 6, P. 444.

192 ELLEN G. WHITE, TESTIMONIES TO MINISTERS AND GOSPEL WORKERS, P. 187.

*laid in ordination, are called to act an important part in soulsaving."*[193]

*"There is a large field open before the self-supporting gospel worker. Many may gain valuable experiences in ministry while toiling a portion of the time at some form of manual labor, and by this method strong workers may be developed for important service in needy fields."*194

4. *"Brethren and sisters, how much work have you done for God during the past year? Do you think that it is those men only who have been ordained as gospel ministers that are to work for the uplifting of humanity? No, no! Everyone who names the name of Christ is expected by God to engage in this work. The hands of ordination may not have been laid upon you, but you are none the less God's messengers. If you have tasted that the Lord is gracious, if you know his saving power, you can no more keep from telling this to some one else than you can keep the wind from blowing. You will have a word in season for him that is weary. You will guide the feet of the straying back to the fold. Your efforts to help others will be untiring, because God's Spirit is working in you."*[195]

5. *"You have neighbors. Will you give them the message? You may never have had the hands of ordination laid upon you, but you can humbly carry the message. You can testify that . . . all for whom Christ died shall have everlasting life if they believe on Him."*[196]

6. *"Let not the work that needs to be done wait for the ordination of ministers. If there are not ministers to take up the work, let men of intelligence, with no thought of how they can accumulate the most property, establish themselves in these cities and towns, and lift up the standard of the cross, using the knowledge they have gained in winning souls to the truth."*[197] *"The knowledge of the truth is altogether too precious to be hoarded up, and bound about, and hid in the earth. Even the one talent entrusted by the Master is to be faithfully employed to gain other talents also. Where are the men and women who have been refreshed with rich streams of blessing from the throne of God? Let them ask themselves what they have done to communicate this light to those who have not had like advantages? How will those who have neglected to use their talents stand in the judgment, when every motive will be brought under scrutiny? The heavenly Master has committed to every one of his servants talents. 'And unto one he gave five talents, to another two, and to another one; to every man according to his several ability.'"*[198]

193 ELLEN G. WHITE, WELFARE MINISTRY, P. 63.

194 IBID., P. 64.

195 ELLEN G. WHITE, IN REVIEW AND HERALD, NOV. 24, 1904.

196 ELLEN G. WHITE, IN HEAVENLY PLACES, P. 323.

197 ELLEN G. WHITE, IN SIGNS OF THE TIMES, JAN. 23, 1893.

198 IBID.

7. *"There are many ways of working for Christ. Human hands may never have been laid on you in ordination, but God can give you fitness for His service. He can work through you to the saving of souls. If, having learned in the school of Christ, you are meek and lowly in heart, He will give you words to speak for Him. Ask, and receive the Holy Spirit. But remember that the Spirit is given only to those who are consecrated, who deny self, lifting the cross and following their Lord."*[199]

Ordination does not give supernatural power:

"The ordination by the laying on of hands was, at a later date, greatly abused; unwarrantable importance was attached to the act, as though a power came at once upon those who received such ordination, which immediately qualified them for any and all ministerial work, as though virtue lay in the act of laying on of hands. We have, in the history of these two apostles, only a simple record of the laying on of hands, and its bearing upon their work. Both Paul and Barnabas had already received their commission from God Himself; and the ceremony of the laying on of hands added no new grace or virtual qualification. It was merely setting the seal of the church upon the work of God - an acknowledged form of designation to an appointed office."[200]

The point here is that the mere act of placing hands on a person does not convey supernatural powers. It is the Spirit that gives power. People on their own do not have power that can be transferred just by the laying on of hands. On the other hand, no one is to be kept back from doing ministry just because hands have not been laid upon them. Ministry is a commission ordained by God Himself to every believer. The natural desire to share the good news springs out of a heart overflowing with love for the Savior that spontaneously and automatically breaks forth in action to share. This torrent of instant effort cannot be circumscribed. The laying on of hands on an individual simply affirms the calling already demonstrated in words and actions. First comes the evidence and then comes the recognition that the man has been called.

---

*199 ELLEN G.WHITE, BIBLE TRAINING SCHOOL, MARCH 1, 1912 PAR. 6}*

*200 ELLEN G.WHITE, THE STORY OF REDEMPTION, P. 304.*

# WOMEN'S ORDINATION - WHITE ESTATE: GENERAL CONFERENCE SESSION 1990

The following information is taken from Appendix C, "Exhibits Relating to the Ordination of Women," in the book Daughters of God. It was "a paper presented at the ministerial meeting at the 1990 General Conference session. Prepared by the White Estate staff." I am including this in this book because its documented history bears on the issue at hand. The remainder of this chapter is taken from the book Daughters of God, pages 248 through 254:

From the Lifetime and Experience of Ellen G. White

1. *A resolution to ordain women was discussed at the general conference of 1881. No action was taken. The minutes include the following lines: "Resolved, that females possessing the necessary qualifications to fill that position may, with perfect propriety, be set apart by ordination to the work of the Christian Ministry.*

*"This was discussed by J. O. Corliss, A. C. Bourdeau, E. R. Jones, D. H. Lamson, W. H. Littlejohn, A. S. Hutchins, D. M. Canright, and J. N. Loughborough, and referred to the General Conference Committee."—The Review and Herald, December 20, 1881.*

*Ellen White did not attend the General Conference of 1881. Her husband died on August 6 of that year. Two weeks after his death she left Battle Creek, bound for California. She did not return to Michigan until August of 1883.*

2. *For many years Ellen White was voted ministerial credentials by the Michigan conference (see, e.g., The Review and Herald, September 10, 1872) and then later by the General Conference. However, she was never ordained by human hands, nor did she ever perform a wedding, organize a church, or conduct a baptism.*

3. *In 1895 Ellen White recommended the ordination of women who would give themselves to a deaconess-type of work:*

*"Women who are willing to consecrate some of their time to the service of the Lord should be appointed to visit the sick, look after the young, and minister to the necessities of the poor. They should be set apart to this work by prayer and laying on of hands. In some cases they will need to counsel with the church officers or the minister; but if they are devoted women, maintaining a vital connection with God, they will be a power for good in the*

*church. This is another means of strengthening and building up the church."—The Review and Herald, July 9, 1895.*

*A number of women were ordained as deaconesses during Ellen White's Australian ministry. On August 10, 1895, the nominating committee at the Ashfield church in Sydney rendered its report, which was approved. The clerk's minutes for that date state: "Immediately following the election, the officers were called to the front where pastors Corliss and McCullagh set apart the elder, deacons, [and] deaconesses by prayer and the laying on of hands."*

*Several years later, in the same church, W. C. White officiated at the ordination of the church officers. The minutes of the Ashfield church for January 7, 1900, state: "The previous Sabbath officers had been nominated and accepted for the current year, and today Elder White ordained and laid hands on the elders, deacon, and deaconesses.—AR, January 16, 1986.*

4. *Women "licensed to preach" by the Seventh-day Adventist Church during Ellen White's lifetime included the following:*

| | | |
|---|---|---|
| *1878* | *Anna Fulton* | *Minnesota* |
| | *Ellen S. Lane* | *Michigan* |
| | *Julia Owen* | *Kentucky-Tennessee* |
| *1879* | *Libbie Collins* | *Minnesota* |
| | *Hattie Enoch* | *Kansas* |
| | *Libbie Fulton* | *Minnesota* |
| | *Lizzie Post* | *Minnesota* |
| *1880* | *Anna Johnson* | *Minnesota* |
| *1881* | *Ida W. Ballenger* | *Illinois* |
| | *Helen L. Morse* | *Illinois* |
| *1884* | *Ruie Hill* | *Kansas* |
| *1886* | *Ida W. Hibben* | *Illinois* |
| *1887* | *Mrs. S. E. Pierce* | *Vermont* |
| *1893* | *Flora Plummer* | *Iowa* |
| *1894* | *Margaret Caro* | *New Zealand* |
| *1895* | *Mrs. S. A. Lindsay* | *New York* |
| *1898* | *Sarepta Irish Henry* | *Gen. Conf.* |
| | *Lulu Wightman* | *New York* |
| *1899* | *Edith Bartlett* | *British Conf.* |
| *1900* | *Hetty Haskell* | *Gen. Conf.* |
| | *Mina Robinson* | *British Conf.* |
| *1901* | *Carrie V. Hansen* | *Utah* |

| | | |
|---|---|---|
| | *Emma Hawkins* | *Iowa* |
| | *Mrs. E. R. Williams* | *Michigan* |
| *1902* | *Mrs. S. N. Haskell* | *Greater NY* |
| | *Minnie Sype* | *Oklahoma* |
| *1904* | *Alma Bjdigg* | *Finland Mission* |
| | *Mrs. J. E. Bond* | *Arizona* |
| | *Bertha E. Jorgensen* | *South Dakota* |
| *1910* | *Pearl Field* | *Nebraska* |
| | *Mrs. Ura Spring* | *Nebraska* |

General Conference Archives and SDA Yearbooks.

Some of the women listed above were employed by the church. Others, such as Margaret Caro, who was a dentist, were self-supporting.

5. *Ellen White made three statements which are sometimes construed as evidence that she supported the concept of women as ordained gospel ministers.*

*In 1898 she declared that "there are women who should labor in the gospel ministry" (Evangelism 472). The context of this statement seems to indicate that she is speaking of ministers' wives. She wrote:*

*"Letters have come to me from several, asking my advice upon the question, Should ministers' wives adopt infant children? Would I advise them to do this kind of work. To some who were regarding this matter favorably, I answered, No; God would have you help your husband in his work. The Lord has not given you children of your own; His wisdom is not to be questioned. He knows what is best. Consecrate your powers to God as a Christian worker. You can help your husband in many ways. . . .*

*"There are women who should labor in the gospel ministry. In many respects they would do more good than the ministers who neglect to visit the flock of God. Husband and wife may unite in this work, and when it is possible, they should. The way is open for consecrated women. But the enemy would be pleased to have the women whom God could use to help hundreds binding up their time and strength on one helpless little mortal that requires constant care and attention."—Manuscript Releases 5:325, 326.*

*In the year 1900 Ellen White published Testimonies, volume 6, which includes a section titled "The Canvasser a Gospel Worker." Here the author states:*

*"All who desire an opportunity for true ministry, and who will give themselves unreservedly to God, will find in the canvassing work opportunities to speak upon many things pertaining to the future, immortal life. The experience thus gained will be of the greatest value to those who are fitting themselves for the ministry. It is the accompaniment of the Holy Spirit of God that prepares workers, both men and women, to become pastors to the flock of God."—Testimonies for the Church 6:322.*

*Finally, in September 1903 Ellen White wrote:*

*"The Lord calls upon those connected with our sanitariums, publishing houses, and schools to teach the youth to do evangelistic work. Our time and energy must not be so largely employed in establishing sanitariums, food stores, and restaurants that other lines of work will be neglected. Young men and young women who should be engaged in the ministry, in Bible work, and in the canvassing work should not be bound down to mechanical employment.*

*"The youth should be encouraged to attend our training schools for Christian workers, which should become more and more like the schools of the prophets. These institutions have been established by the Lord, and if they are conducted in harmony with His purpose, the youth sent to them will quickly be prepared to engage in various lines of missionary work. Some will be trained to enter the field as missionary nurses, some as canvassers, and some as gospel ministers."—Testimonies for the Church 8:229, 230.*

6. *Ellen White made two statements about her own call to serve the Lord as his messenger. She declared:*

*"At the age of 78 I am still toiling. We are all in the hands of the Lord. I trust in Him; for I know that He will never leave nor forsake those who put their trust in Him. I have committed myself to His keeping.*

*"And I thank Christ Jesus our Lord, who hath enabled me, for that He counted me faithful, putting me into the ministry."—The Review and Herald, July 26, 1906.*

*"In the city of Portland the Lord ordained me as His messenger, and here my first labors were given to the cause of present truth."—The Review and Herald, May 18, 1911.*

*It will be recalled that Ellen White was given her first vision in December 1844, in Portland, Maine. Shortly thereafter she was prompted by the Lord to tell others what she had seen.*

7. *Ellen White did not concern herself with women's rights movements. When she*

*was urged to join others in the crusade for women's suffrage, she declined the invitation. She wrote to her husband:*

*"I called upon Mrs. Graves. She had a burden upon her mind and ever since she knew I was at home she desired to see me. She said she felt that she must talk out her feelings to me. She is desirous that women's suffrage should be looked into by me. She says women ought to vote, and she related many things of a startling character which were legalized in France and St. Louis, and an effort was made to carry them out in Chicago this year, but [the effort] failed. Houses of ill fame are legalized. Women who travel alone through those cities, if they are the least suspicious of them, are taken up by the authorities and their cases are investigated. If they are diseased they are placed in the care of the doctors and cured. Then they are fit for the visits of men and are placed in the legalized home for men to satisfy their lusts upon. No examination is made of the men, and where this law is carried into effect the crime and immorality resemble the condition of the world which existed previous to the flood."*

*"Mrs. Graves viewed the matter as I do in regard to the increase of crime and demoralization of society. She says women must vote if this law is [to be] withstood. We had a long talk in regard to temperance. I told her that my mind was unprepared for any such matter as women voting. She had been thinking and dwelling upon these things and her mind was ripe upon them, while my work was of another character. We were doing upon the point of temperance what no other class of people in the world were. We were as much in favor of a pledge against tobacco as liquor."—Manuscript Releases 10:69.*

*8. It is likely that Ellen White did not suggest at any time that the Seventh-day Adventist Church should commence the practice of ordaining women to the gospel ministry. Her secretary, C. C. Crisler, says that she was very cautious on this point. Here is the correspondence relating to this question:*

*"March 12, 1916*
*"Mr. Clarence Crisler, Sanitarium [California]*
*"Dear brother:*
*"Will you please inform me in regard to the setting apart of women who can give some time to missionary work, by laying on hands in prayer, found in Review and Herald, back in the early part of the nineties, probably back in about 1892 or 1893, from the pen of Sister White.*

*"The reason I ask for this, I was in a recent meeting where Elder Andross set aside women by the laying on of hands, and when I asked him for the authority for so doing, he referred me to you, and as I have been a Bible worker for a number of years and have recently been granted a ministerial license, I want this information.*

*"Please answer at once, as I want to hear from you before I go to the Southwestern Union Conference, which convenes April 7. Please send me two or three copies of her statement, as the president of our conference wants one."—Mrs. L. E. Cox, 134 Agarita Avenue, San Antonio, Texas.*

*"March 22, 1916*

*"Mrs. L. E. Cox, San Antonio, Texas*

*"Dear sister,*

*"I have your letter of the twelfth, making inquiry regarding the ordination of women who give some time to missionary work—particularly to some statement which you believe to be found in a Review early in the nineties, from the pen of Mrs. Ellen G.White.*

*"As this query will require some study on my part, and searching, and as I must go to Mountain View in the morning for a few days, I am under the necessity of asking that you excuse me from answering for a few days. Upon my return, early next week, I will endeavor to send you a reply, accompanying same, if possible, with the extracts called for. However, I might say that I have not understood these extracts as teaching positively the ordination of women as ministers of the gospel. I have supposed, rather, that they refer primarily to the ordination of God-fearing women as deaconesses in local churches. But of this I will speak more fully when I write again.*

*"I hope to write you about the twenty-eighth, and will address you as above. If you are leaving San Antonio for other parts, it would be well for you to leave a forwarding order, so mail addressed as above will reach you in due time at the Union Conference."*

*- Clarence Crisler.*

*"June 16, 1916*

*"Mrs. L. E. Cox*

*"Dear sister,*

*"In my answer under date of March 22, I was unable to forward you copy of the Review article called for, but ventured to say, 'I have not understood these extracts as teaching positively the ordination of women as ministers of the gospel. I have supposed, rather, that they refer primarily to the ordination of God-fearing women as deaconesses in local churches.'*

*"Since writing the above, I have found the article in question and have had same copied. Enclosed find a copy of this article. [The Review and Herald, July 9, 1895.] I am also forwarding a copy to your local Conference president, Elder E. L. Neff, and to the president of your Union, Elder J.W. Christian, that they may know what I am sending to you.*

*"While I do not make it a part of my work to presume to interpret that which has been written, yet I may be pardoned for expressing as my conviction the thought that this article published in the Review does not refer to the ordination of women as ministers of*

*the gospel, but rather touches upon the question of setting apart, for special duties in local churches, God-fearing women in such churches where circumstances call for such action.*

*"And may I add that Sister White, personally, was very careful about expressing herself in any wise as to the advisability of ordaining women as gospel ministers. She has often spoken of the perils that such general practice would expose the church to by a gainsaying world; but as yet I have never seen from her pen any statement that would seem to encourage the formal and official ordination of women to the gospel ministry, to public labor such as is ordinarily expected of an ordained minister.*

*"This is not suggesting, much less saying, that no women are fitted for such public labor, and that none should ever be ordained; it is simply saying that so far as my knowledge extends, Sister White never encouraged church officials to depart from the general customs of the church in those matters."—C. C. Crisler.*

### Conclusion

The question of women's ordination was not high on Ellen White's agenda during her lifetime. Her best energies were directed toward achieving a greater unity and a deeper spirituality in the church.

## THE ROLE OF WOMEN IN THE CHURCH

Seventh-day Adventists adhere to the belief that the Bible is the only Guidebook necessary for the basis of faith and practice for the believing Christian. Yet, unlike many of their Protestant counterparts, Adventists also believe that the biblical gift of prophecy, by which the prophets could receive heavenly instruction (see Amos 3:7), would continue to be imparted until the end of time. Its role would provide for the "perfecting of the saints, for the work of the ministry, for the edifying of the body of Christ: Till we all come in the unity of the faith, and of the knowledge of the Son of God, unto a perfect man, unto the measure of the stature of the fullness of Christ: that we henceforth be no more children, tossed to and fro, and carried about with every wind of doctrine, by the sleight of men, and cunning craftiness, whereby they lie in wait to deceive" (Ephesians 4:12-14).

This prophetic gift to the church was manifested in the life and work of Ellen G. White, who lived from 1827 to 1915. The canonization of the Scriptures precludes any addendum to it. Hence, any post revelations are subject to be scrutinized for their validity or fallacy by the Bible. Therefore, any future acclaimed prophetic gift does not supersede or become an addition to the Sacred Canon. "In light of its belief in the prophetic role of Ellen White, the church takes her writings seriously, viewing them as a source of 'comfort, guidance, instruction, and correction.'"[201] Just as believers do not believe in Paul, but rather in the counsels God gave through him, so Adventists do not believe in Ellen White, but rather in the counsels that God gave through her.

Because the issue of ordination of women has become paramount in the minds of many, her writings have become a hopeful arsenal for ammunition to support each of the opposing views. The question that surfaces is What was Ellen White's stance in regard to the ordination of women to the gospel ministry? It is not surprising that the variety of ideas and opinions about what stance she held on this issue has been accompanied by differing constructions of what her position was.

The majority of researchers have focused more in finding support for women's ordination in Ellen White's writings or in her involvement in the Adventist Church's history. Because of this fact, it is important to examine the validity of claims that suggest her support in favor of women's ordination. Let us briefly look at what Ellen White taught regarding the ministry of women in the church.

In 1895 Ellen White made a statement relative to the ordination of women. The statement reads: "Women who are willing to consecrate some of their time to the service of the Lord should be appointed to visit the sick, look after the young, and minister to the necessities of the poor. They should be set apart to this work by prayer and laying on of hands. In some cases they will need to counsel with

---

201 *ADVENT REVIEW AND SABBATH HERALD (HEREINAFTER REVIEW AND HERALD OR SIMPLY REVIEW) JULY 9, 1895.*

the church officers or the minister; but if they are devoted women, maintaining a vital connection with God, they will be a power for good in the church. This is another means of strengthening and building up the church. We need to branch out more in our methods of labor. Not a hand should be bound, not a soul discouraged, not a voice should be hushed; let every individual labor, privately or publicly, to help forward this grand work. Place the burdens upon men and women of the church, that they may grow by reason of the exercise, and thus become effective agents in the hand of the Lord for the enlightenment of those who sit in darkness."[202]

This statement recommends that women should "be set apart to this work by prayer and laying on of hands." Since the counsel is to ordain them, the question is, for what? Let us dissect the statement to determine the answer.

1. *"Women who are willing to consecrate some of their time . . ."This is part-time labor. There is no suggestion that these women enter into full-time pastoral work.*

2. *"Be appointed to visit the sick, look after the young, and minister to the necessities of the poor." The tasks were specific and limited in nature.*

3. *"In some cases they will need to counsel with the church officers or the minister." There is no mention that they necessarily held church positions. Apparently, this was auxiliary in nature, "appointed" to contribute to special needs in consultation with the "church officers or the minister."*

4. *"In some cases they will need to counsel with the church officers or the minister." They are not equated with the minister or church officers who had the responsibility of leading the congregation.*

5. *"This is another means of strengthening and building up the church. We need to branch out more in our methods of labor. Not a hand should be bound, not a soul discouraged, not a voice should be hushed; let every individual labor, privately or publicly, to help forward this grand work."The encouragement was intended to provide other areas of involvement in the work of the Lord. Delegation apparently was lacking and areas of the work were being unattended to by the officers or ministers.*

---

202 *ELLEN G. WHITE, IN REVIEW AND HERALD, JULY 9, 1895.*

6. *"Place the burdens upon men and women of the church, that they may grow by reason of the exercise, and thus become effective agents in the hand of the Lord." This was lay work intended to open opportunity for the members to grow spiritually by doing service for the Lord.*

From careful observation of her statement it becomes clear that Ellen White was not calling for the ordination of a woman to the ministry. The statement clearly distinguishes this "setting aside" from that of the minister or the church officers. To suggest that Ellen White in this statement supports ordaining women to pastoral positions or leadership of congregations or ecclesiastical authority is simply not supported by the quote cited.

The statement in question is found in the article entitled "The Duty of the Minister and the People." The article was another clarion call to the ministers and officers of the church to quit hoarding the work and encourage the men and women comprising the church to take ownership of the Lord's labors. "Its purpose is not to change the structure of the pastoral ministry, but rather to change its emphasis from one in which most of the burdens are seized and carried by the minister, to one in which the laity is active and motivated in the work of the church."[203]

In the article this is plainly seen as she continues to address these women in relationship to the work and the pastor: "The minister's work is the lay member's work as well. Heart should be bound to heart. Let all press forward, shoulder to shoulder. Is not every true follower of Christ open to receive his teachings? And should not all have an opportunity to learn of Christ's methods by practical experience? Why not put them to work visiting the sick and assisting in other ways, and thus keep the church in a workable condition? All would thus be kept in close touch with the minister's plans, so that he could call for their assistance at any moment, and they would be able to labor intelligently with him. All should be laborers together with God, and then the minister can feel that he has helpers in whom it is safe to trust. The minister can hasten this desirable end by showing

---

203 *WILLIAM FAGAL, THE ROLE OF WOMEN IN THE CHURCH (1987).*

that he has confidence in the workers by setting them to work,"[204]

In support of this issue some have taken several statements and linked them together as proof of Ellen White's favor for women's ordination. The one says: "Women should be educated and qualified just as thoroughly as possible to become practitioners in the delicate diseases which afflict women, that their secret parts should not be exposed to the notice of men. There should be a much larger number of lady physicians, educated not only to act as trained nurses, but also as physicians."205 The next one reads: "The ordained ministers alone are not equal to the task. God is calling not only upon the ministers, but also upon physicians, nurses, canvassers, Bible workers, and other consecrated laymen of varied talent who have a knowledge of present truth, to consider the needs of the unwarned cities."[206]

The following one is where the matter of setting aside for a physician is recommended. It reads: "The work of the true medical missionary is largely a spiritual work. It includes prayer and the laying on of hands; he therefore should be as sacredly set apart for his work as is the minister of the gospel. Those who are selected to act the part of missionary physicians, are to be set apart as such. This will strengthen them against the temptation to withdraw from the sanitarium work to engage in private practice. No selfish motives should be allowed to draw the worker from his post of duty. We are living in a time of solemn responsibilities; a time when consecrated work is to be done. Let us seek the Lord diligently and understandingly."[207]

Do these statements mandate the ordination of a male or female physician as a pastor? If Ellen White had intended that, she would not have used indirect language. In harmony with her manner, she would have plainly stated, "Set him apart as a minister." However, the language is clear: "He therefore should be as sacredly set apart

---

*204 ELLEN G.WHITE, IN REVIEW AND HERALD, JULY 9, 1895.*

*205 ELLEN G.WHITE, COUNSELS ON HEALTH, P. 364.*

*206 ELLEN G.WHITE, MEDICAL MINISTRY, P. 248.*

*207 ELLEN G.WHITE, MANUSCRIPT RELEASES, VOL. 1, P. 73.*

for his work," but not as a minister, rather as a "missionary physician." Obviously the temptation existed for those trained in medical lines to go into private practice to make money. So in order to "strengthen them against the temptation to withdraw from" the gospel work as a missionary at the sanitarium, ordination was encouraged. This would lift their medical work to the spiritual level as that of the ministers.

In reference to the sacred labors of the medical missionary she said this work "includes prayer and the laying on of hands."[208] While it is true that this phrase can easily be misconstrued to be in reference to ordination, the stronger weight of evidence suggests that the physicians being set aside would necessitate them laying on hands and praying for the sick. In the Bible the phrase "laying on of hands" did not always translate into ordination. Besides ordaining His disciples, Jesus laid hands on children to bless them (see Matthew 19:13, 15), and to heal the sick (see Luke 4:40, 13:13). Therefore, in both the Scriptures and the writings of Ellen White the expression "prayer and the laying on of hands" is not limited to one definition. The context must be considered.

Once again we can see that this passage will not support the claim that Ellen White called for women to be ordained into the pastoral ministry.

There is no question that Ellen White was emphatic that women should labor in the gospel ministry. She wrote, "There are women who should labor in the gospel ministry. In many respects they would do more good than the ministers who neglect to visit the flock of God."[209] She even suggested that women were to be paid fairly for their work from the tithe: "The tithe should go to those who labor in word and doctrine, be they men or women."[210]

The conclusion that some have come to in reference to these statements is that she is eliminating role distinction between men

---

208 *Ellen White, Evangelism, p. 547.*

209 *Ellen G. White, Manuscript Releases, vol. 5, p. 325.*

210 *Ellen G. White, Manuscript Releases, vol. 1, p. 262.*

and women in the ministry. Yet fairness in pay and being paid from the tithe does not necessarily mean ordination. Notice the following statement: "These women give their whole time, and are told that they receive nothing for their labors because their husbands receive wages. I tell them to go forward and all such decisions will be revised. The Word says, 'The laborer is worthy of his hire.' Luke 10:7. When any such decision as this is made, I will, in the name of the Lord, protest. I will feel it my duty to create a fund from my tithe money to pay these women who are accomplishing just as essential work as the ministers are doing, and this tithe I will reserve for work in the same line as that of the ministers, hunting for souls, fishing for souls. I know that the faithful women should be paid wages as it is considered proportionate to the pay received by ministers. They carry the burden of souls and should not be treated unjustly. These sisters are giving their time to educating those newly come to the faith and hire their own work done and pay those who work for them. All these things must be adjusted and set in order and justice be done to all."[211]

"The ministers are paid for their work, and this is well. And if the Lord gives the wife, as well as the husband, the burden of labor, and if she devotes her time and her strength to visiting from family to family, opening the Scriptures to them, although the hands of ordination have not been laid upon her, she is accomplishing a work that is in the line of ministry. Should her labors be counted as naught, and her husband's salary be no more than that of the servant of God whose wife does not give herself to the work, but remains at home to care for her family?"[212]

The matter of using tithe for different ministries was clearly taught by Ellen White. In reference to using the tithe for medical missionary work, she wrote: "If this money in tithe is paid by the workers into the treasury, why, I ask, should not that amount be apportioned to the carrying forward of the medical missionary work?—Letter 51a, 1898, p. 1. (To Uriah Smith and G. A. Irwin, June 6, 1898.)"[213]

---

211 *ELLEN G. WHITE, DAUGHTERS OF GOD, P. 106.*

212 *ELLEN G. WHITE, MANUSCRIPT RELEASES, VOL., 5, P. 29.*

213 *ELLEN G. WHITE, MANUSCRIPT RELEASES, VOL. 7, P. 366.*

Tithe was also used to pay Bible teachers. "Light has been plainly given that those who minister in our schools, teaching the Word of God, explaining the Scriptures, educating the students in the things of God, should be supported by the tithe money."[214]

The inference is also made that, because of her insistence that women should be treated fairly, Ellen White clearly intends that ordination must be done irrespective of gender. This conclusion is not supported at all in the above statements, for she clearly says: "although the hands of ordination have not been laid upon her."

Part of the problem contributing to this dilemma is simply the misunderstanding in regard to the phrase "gospel ministry." Notice what she says is ministry: "educating those newly come to the faith." "If she devotes her time and her strength to visiting from family to family, opening the Scriptures to them, although the hands of ordination have not been laid upon her, she is accomplishing a work that is in the line of ministry." Ellen White is not using the phrase "gospel ministry" in the sense of women performing a role of being a pastor, but rather a function of service in ministering to others' needs, be it spiritual or physical.

The issue she was addressing was the injustices being done to the women who labored for souls, but were not being remunerated accordingly. And by so doing, they were discouraging the women from doing what the ministers should have been doing and were not, resulting in an important aspect of the work left undone. There is no question that the church has been gravely at fault in this area of fairness toward women. Nevertheless, correcting the matter does not require going beyond what Ellen White had both explicitly and implicitly stated.

It is important to note Ellen White's insight into the skills necessary for the work and the edge that women had for personal soul winning. The need for additional workers was in part also created by the negligence of the paid ministers in doing personal work.

---

*214 ELLEN G.WHITE, COUNSELS OF STEWARDSHIP, P. 103.*

Relative to this point she wrote: "Those who go forth as ministers have a solemn responsibility devolving upon them which is strangely neglected. Some enjoy preaching, but they do not give personal labor to the churches."[215] For this reason she made the statement: "In many respects they would do more good than the ministers who neglect to visit the flock of God."

"You [she suggested to the brethren] are to do your duty to the women who labor in the gospel, whose work testifies that they are essential to carry the truth into families. Their work is just the work that must be done. In many respects a woman can impart knowledge to her sisters that a man cannot. The cause would suffer great loss without this kind of labor. Again and again the Lord has shown me that women teachers are just as greatly needed to do the work to which He has appointed them as are men. They should not be compelled by the sentiments and rules of others to depend upon donations for their payment, any more than should the ministers."[216] There is no question that if more devoted women were involved in this work, the Lord's coming would undoubtedly be hastened.

I should hasten also to mention that the prophet was not excluding the males from the work or suggesting that men and women exchange roles. Rather, she recommended that a combined effort would be more efficacious: "Husband and wife may unite in this work, and when it is possible, they should. The way is open for consecrated women."[217]

Ellen White felt strongly about injustices done against certain women that she was personally acquainted with who were not getting remunerated for their labors. In addressing her concerns she named some of the women. She wrote: "There are ministers' wives—Sisters Starr, Haskell, Wilson, and Robinson—who have been devoted, earnest, whole-souled workers, giving Bible readings and praying with families, helping along by personal efforts just as successfully as their

215 *IBID., P. 104.*

216 *ELLEN G. WHITE, MANUSCRIPT RELEASES, VOL. 5, P. 325.*

217 *ELLEN G. WHITE, DAUGHTERS OF GOD, PP. 202, 203.*

husbands. These women give their whole time, and are told that they receive nothing for their labors because their husbands receive wages. I tell them to go forward and all such decisions will be revised. The Word says, "The labourer is worthy of his hire." Luke 10:7. When any such decision as this is made, I will, in the name of the Lord, protest. I will feel it my duty to create a fund from my tithe money to pay these women who are accomplishing just as essential work as the ministers are doing, and this tithe I will reserve for work in the same line as that of the ministers, hunting for souls, fishing for souls."[218]

As can be seen, while she recognizes that the work of the ministers should be remunerated, she stresses the need to also have their wives paid who are laboring side by side with their husbands to do the kind of work she envisioned women doing. It was a special work of gospel ministry for women and families. This work entailed personal work of home visitation, giving Bible studies, and encouraging the believers. The women mentioned were all ministers' wives, who could, in her estimation, make the work of their husbands complete by filling the void they were not able, or neglected, to do.

Not long ago, a former student of mine, who is working as a full-time minister, sent a statement to me and asked for an explanation. Since I had not seen the statement before, I took time to study, research, and communicate with the White Estate to ascertain its meaning. The statement read as follows: "All who wish an opportunity for true ministry, and who will give themselves unreservedly to God, will find in the canvassing work opportunities to speak upon many things pertaining to the future immortal life. The experience thus gained will be of the greatest value to those who are fitting themselves for work of the ministry. It is the accompaniment of the Holy Spirit of God that prepares workers, both men and women, to become pastors to the flock of God."[219] This statement appeared in an article entitled "Canvassers as Gospel Evangelists" in the January 15, 1901, edition of the Review and Herald.

---

*218 IBID., P. 106.*

*219 ELLEN G.WHITE, "CANVASSERS AS GOSPEL EVANGELISTS," REVIEW AND HERALD," JAN. 15, 1901.*

More than two years prior, in 1898, Ellen White wrote: "There are women who should labor in the gospel ministry. In many respects they would do more good than the ministers who neglect to visit the flock of God. Husband and wife may unite in this work, and when it is possible, they should. The way is open for consecrated women. But the enemy would be pleased to have the women whom God could use to help hundreds, binding up their time and strength on one helpless little mortal, that requires constant care and attention."[220] In this statement she is writing about adopting babies. And by doing so, women with special spiritual abilities who could serve and, when possible accompanied by their husbands, visit the "flock of God" would be hindered.

The statement from "Canvassers as Gospel Evangelists" was written to encourage both men and women to take up that work. By visiting the homes individuals would serve as "pastors to the flock of God." This did not mean that colporteurs would be ordained ministers. Instead, colporteurs would, by home visitation, do the function of pastoring the flock of God and, by so doing, be spiritually benefitting themselves. Here is another statement confirming her use of the word "pastor" in reference to lay people: "Responsibilities must be laid upon the members of the church. The missionary spirit should be awakened as never before, and workers should be appointed as needed, who will act as pastors to the flock, putting forth personal effort to bring the church up to that condition where spiritual life and activity will be seen in all her borders."[221] Her concern was for the personal care of the flock. She enjoined this responsibility on both ministers and laypeople: on men and women.

Part of the challenge during the early days of the Adventist Church is that the minister was more of an evangelist. His work was primarily to go from town to town or city to city, and raise up churches. Once a church was established, he was to turn the work over to the lay workers for the work of "pastoring" the members, while he moved on to the next place to plant another church. In

---

220 *ELLEN G.WHITE, MANUSCRIPT RELEASES, VOL. 5, P. 325.*

221 *ELLEN G.WHITE, TESTIMONIES FOR THE CHURCH, VOL. 5, P. 723.*

many parts of the world, outside of the United States, pastors may have a dozen churches or more. His work of pastoring is very limited. Given the broad range of his responsibilities, he must rely on the elders and leaders of the churches to carry on the work of pastoring the flocks. The elders and other leaders give in-home Bible studies, visit the members, and prepare candidates for baptism. They function as undershepherds. When it is time for a board meeting or they have candidates for baptism, they contact the pastor and request his presence to preside over the board or baptize those prepared, as well as handle disciplinary problems, take care of church business, counsel members, or whatever else needs to be taken care of by the pastor. Otherwise, the experienced men and women of the church do the work of nurturing or pastoring in the sense that Ellen White referred to.

The current practice of pastors hovering over a congregation is a new innovation. In 1901 she began to see this encroaching practice and to curtail it she wrote: "As I traveled through the South on my way to the conference, I saw city after city that was unworked. What is the matter? The ministers are hovering over churches which know the truth while thousands are perishing out of Christ. If the proper instruction were given, if the proper methods were followed, every church member would do his work as a member of the body. He would do Christian missionary work. But the churches are dying, and they want a minister to preach to them."[222]

When it came to her views as to who should be called to enter the actual pastoral ministry as a role, she wrote: "There is an urgent demand for laborers in the gospel field. Young men are needed for this work; God calls for them. Their education is of primary importance in our colleges, and in no case should it be ignored or regarded as a secondary matter. It is entirely wrong for teachers, by suggesting other occupations, to discourage young men who might be qualified to do acceptable work in the ministry. Those who present hindrances to prevent young men from fitting themselves for this work are counterworking the plans of God, and they will have to give

---

222 ELLEN G. WHITE, *EVANGELISM*, P. 381.

an account of their course. There is among us more than an average of men of ability. If their capabilities were brought into use, we should have twenty ministers where we now have one."[223]

In another statement she wrote: "Our College stands today in a position that God does not approve. I have been shown the dangers that threaten this important institution. If its responsible men seek to reach the world's standard, if they copy the plans and methods of other colleges, the frown of God will be upon our school. The time has come for me to speak decidedly. The purpose of God in the establishment of our College has been plainly stated. There is an urgent demand for laborers in the gospel field. Young men who design to enter the ministry cannot spend a number of years in obtaining an education. Teachers should have been able to comprehend the situation and adapt their instruction to the wants of this class. Special advantages should have been given them for a brief yet comprehensive study of the branches most needed to fit them for their work. But I have been shown that this has not been accomplished."[224]

After all that Ellen White wrote about women and their need to be involved in ministry, when it comes to her burden for the need of more candidates for the pastoral ministry, she only mentions men. She clearly believes pastors should be of the male gender. This view is further undergirded in chapter 3 (entitled "The Needed Preparation: Young Men in the Ministry") of her book Gospel Workers. Among the numerous calls for the pastoral ministry as an office, there is no mention of women being encouraged or urged to be among the "young men," or "men" to consider ministry.

The statement from "Canvassers as Gospel Evangelists" that says, "accompaniment of the Holy Spirit of God that prepares workers, both men and women, to become pastors to the flock of God," must be seen in the light of how Ellen White used the word "pastors." Was she actually calling for both men and women to become pastors in the sense of being ordained ministers? Or was she calling for

---

*223 ELLEN G. WHITE, TESTIMONIES FOR THE CHURCH, VOL. 6, P. 135.*

*224 ELLEN G. WHITE, TESTIMONY FOR THE BATTLE CREEK CHURCH (PAMPHLET 117), P. 9.*

canvassers who could do the personal ministry of visitation to give encouragement and Bible instruction? Because she used the word "pastor" to describe an office as well as a function, it leaves the phrase open to an alternative understanding. The "pastors to the flock of God" designates those who exercise a personal ministry of visitation and instruction in the home. If this alternative explanation is chosen, then the statement is congruent with other statements she makes in regard to the complementary work women are especially gifted to do in stride with men.

Ellen White's recommendation is also completely in harmony with the numerous calls she made specifically for males to enter ministerial full-time labor. Those who interpret her statement in support of women becoming pastors would be hard-pressed to support this rationale for the reason this sole statement is in contradiction to all her other statements that clearly support the opposite view.

The servant of the Lord always encouraged both young men and young women to get involved in some aspect of the Lord's work. She wrote: "Young men and young women who should be engaged in the ministry, in Bible work, and in the canvassing work should not be bound down to mechanical employment."[225] While at first glance it appears as if she is encouraging both genders to do ministry, a closer look clarifies what kind of ministry. The burden of the statement is not focusing on which particular aspect of the work is to be done by which gender, but rather that the workers who are being trained at the institution should not be "bound down to mechanical employment." In doing so, the workers would be kept back from doing whatever ministry they are supposed to be engaged in.

The burden of getting the Word out to lost souls was constantly on Ellen White's heart and mind. To encourage more involvement on the part of women who she saw could do much more than they were, she wrote in an 1879 published article: "Women can be the instruments of righteousness, rendering holy service. It was Mary that first preached a risen Jesus. In fulfillment of the divine plan, the

---

*225 ELLEN G.WHITE, IN REVIEW AND HERALD, MAY 16, 1912.*

Son of man came to seek and to save that which was lost. If this work was not beneath the dignity of the world's Redeemer, the Creator of worlds, should it be considered too humiliating for sinful mortals? If Christ taught, and if he wrestled in earnest prayer to his Father in behalf of those he came to save, we should engage in the same work. Those who engage with the Son of God in his work, be they ever so aspiring, can have no greater, no holier work than this. If there were twenty women where now there is one, who would make this holy mission their cherished work, we should see many more converted to the truth. The refining, softening influence of Christian women is needed in the great work of preaching the truth. The Lord of the vineyard is saying to many women who are now doing nothing, 'Why stand ye here all the day idle?' Zealous and continued diligence in our sisters toiling for the spread of the truth would be wholly successful, and would astonish us with its results. Through patience and perseverance, the work must be accomplished. In this faithful work is manifested the real devotion to God. He calls for deeds, and not words only."[226]

She stood amazed at the lack of women bearing the burden of advancing the gospel. Notice that she quotes the Bible: "Why stand ye here all the day idle?" (Matthew 20:6). By comparing them to what Mary did in proclaiming a risen Savior, she alluded to the work women could be doing in emulating her. She wasn't suggesting that Mary was a pastor, rather that she preached the good news of the resurrection. In this sense she stated, "If there were twenty women where now there is one, who would make this holy mission their cherished work, we should see many more converted to the truth. The refining, softening influence of Christian women is needed in the great work of preaching the truth."

In this writing to Mrs. Henry and published in Mrs. Henry's column in the Review, Ellen White wrote: "The work you are doing to help our sisters feel their individual accountability to God is a good and necessary work. Long has it been neglected; but when this work has been laid out in clear lines, simple and definite, we may expect

---

*226 ELLEN G.WHITE, IN REVIEW AND HERALD, JAN. 2, 1879.*

that the essential duties of the home, instead of being neglected, will be done much more intelligently. The Lord would ever have us urge upon those who do not understand, the worth of the human soul."[227] Promoting the employment of women as ministers in the usual sense of the term is not what was intended in the statement. Instead she was clearly encouraging Mrs. Henry to "teach our sisters that every day the question is to be, Lord, what wilt thou have me to do this day?" "If we can arrange, as you are now working, to have regularly organized companies intelligently instructed in regard to the part they should act as servants of the Master, our churches will have life and vitality such as have been so long needed."[228] She encouraged Mrs. Henry to extend her influence by addressing "the crowd whenever you can." Please note that Ellen White's encouragement for speaking is to enable the extension of her influence through that avenue.

"In 1898 she [Mrs. Henry] conceived a plan for what she called 'woman ministry.' Lecturing on the role of the mother in the moral education of society, she stressed this from coast to coast in the United States and Canada. She also presented her plan to SDA congregations. A. W. Spalding remarked later that in the work instituted in the SDA Church by Mrs. Henry came 'the first semblance of an organized effort to train parents and to give help in their problems.'"[229]

Some have used the argument that Ellen White had a ministerial credential. The assertion is that because she was issued a credential, and since only ordained ministers received such credentials, she must have been ordained. One administrator even pulled out a copy of her credentials and showed it to me. Since this is a point of contention, it would serve us well to do a historical analysis of the material.

There is no record to support that Ellen White was ever ordained. It is true that she was granted "ministerial credentials" by various church organizations from 1871 until her death. Three of her credential certificates from the mid-1880s are still in the possession

227 *ELLEN G.WHITE, IN REVIEW AND HERALD, MAY 9, 1899.*

228 *IBID.*

229 *WILLIAM FAGAL, THE ROLE OF WOMEN IN THE CHURCH, (1987).*

of the White Estate in Silver Spring, Maryland. The 1885 certificate issued to her used the title "ordained minister." However, the word "ordained" has a line drawn over it.

Two years later (1887) she was issued another credential, and this time the word "ordination" was not struck. This has led some to the conclusion that she must have been ordained in the interim. But if that had been the case, then the question would have to be raised as to why she was voted ordained minster's credentials for the previous 15 years without being ordained. The truth is that this cannot be used as proof, because in the certificate of 1883 the word "ordained" had not been crossed out. This certificate is also in the possession of the White Estate.

Since the word "ordained" was crossed out in 1885, one could surmise that during the succeeding two years, until the reissuing of the 1887 credential, she was somehow working in an "unordained" status. It is also quite possible that the issuers of the credentials in 1885 issued her the credential, which gave the bearer the authenticity of being a denominational worker, while at the same time making the statement that she was not ordained. Something of the sort could have been the case, since there is no evidence that such a credential without the word "ordained" exists.

What is interesting is that she served the church as a prophet without credentials for 25 years prior to 1871. But as the church grew and more workers were added to its working force, it became necessary for the church to single out and validate its workers by issuing credentials. Therefore, it became necessary for the church to officially validate Ellen White's standing with the church. "One clear evidence of the church's confidence in her work is that, recognizing her ordination by God and not man, she was given ministerial credentials by the General Conference, the highest authority in the church."[230]

Ellen White personally settled the issue concerning whether

---

*230 "A WORD ON BEHALF OF ELLEN WHITE AS A PERSON," A CRITIQUE OF THE BOOK PROPHETESS OF HEALTH, P. 93.*

or not she was ordained. In 1909 she filled out a "Biographical Information Blank" for the General Conference records. "The question, 'When, where, and in what capacity did you begin laboring in the cause?' is answered, 'In Maine, 1842, laboring for young friends; 1844-1845 began public labors, relating visions, etc.' A simple 'X' is the only mark in the two lines allotted for information 'If ordained, state when, where, and by whom.' Down through the years, in yearbooks and General Conference bulletins, her name appears with the 'ordained ministers.' On her periodically issued ministerial credentials the word ordained was at times neatly crossed out, at other times standing. Her brethren were faced with a dilemma. Since she was uniquely and unquestionably ordained by God as he had laid his hand upon her, it would be anticlimactic were men to set her apart to the ministry by 'the laying on of hands.' At no time did she perform those functions reserved to the ordained minister."[231]

Notice that on the question "If ordained, state when, where, and by whom," she has simply inscribed an X. She did the same when asked, "If remarried, give date, and to whom." The reason for the X simply meant that it did not apply. She was never ordained, and she never remarried.

Roger Coon, in addressing the topic of Ellen White and ordination, wrote: "EGW was herself never ordained to the gospel ministry by human hands. She held the credentials of an ordained minister, first from the Michigan Conference and later from the General Conference (on one of the certificates, the word 'ordained' is crossed out by the stroke of a pen; on some it is not—they were issued every year).

Following the death of her husband, James White, in 1881, she was paid the salary of an ordained minister. She never performed tasks usually associated with a minister: (1) Weddings, (2) Baptisms, (3) Organization of churches."[232]

---

231 *ARTHUR L.WHITE, TABLE OF CONTENTS, EDITOR'S NOTE, ELLEN G.WHITE THE PERSON.*

232 *ROGER W. COON, "EGW AND THE QUESTION OF ORDINATION OF WOMEN," ELLEN G. WHITE'S VIEW OF THE ROLE OF WOMEN IN THE SDA CHURCH, P. 8.*

Part of the problem contributing to the matter of women's ordination is the issue of headship. Contrary to the positions currently taken by some in favor of women's ordination, Ellen White was crystal clear on the topic of the headship. She upheld, in her practice and teaching, the Bible's statements on the headship of the husband in marriage. In a letter written to a friend in her early married life, she wrote: "We women must remember that God has placed us subject to the husband. He is the head and our judgment and views and reasonings must agree with his if possible. If not, the preference in God's Word is given to the husband where it is not a matter of conscience. We must yield to the head."[233] Concerning family difficulty she counseled: "They [the husband and wife] should have a united interest in all that concerns their homemaking, and the wife, if a Christian, will have her interest with her husband as his companion; for the husband is to stand as the head of the household."[234]

In her labors Ellen White had strong convictions about her relationship to the pulpit. "She would not stand in the pulpit to speak at the Sabbath morning worship service if James White was present. He would take the Sabbath morning service, and she would speak in the afternoon. Only when he was stricken with paralysis in 1865 and for some time could not take his place in public work did she depart from this procedure."[235] Here is another statement: "Finally the first Sabbath of the session arrived to break the busy routine. D. T. Bourdeau spoke Sabbath morning at the worship service, with Sister White occupying the pulpit in the afternoon."[236]

In 1902 Ellen White wrote: "They [women] may take their places in his work at this crisis, and he [the Lord] will work through them. If they are imbued with a sense of their duty, and labor under the influence of the Holy Spirit, they will have just the self-possession required for this time. The Saviour will reflect upon these self-sacrificing

---

233 *ELLEN G. WHITE, LETTER 5, 1861, P. 2. (TO MRS. J. N. LOUGHBOROUGH, JUNE 6, 1861.)*

234 *ELLEN G. WHITE, THE ADVENTIST HOME, P. 119.*

235 *ARTHUR L. WHITE, ELLEN WHITE THE PERSON, P. 10.*

236 *D. A. DELAFIELD, ELLEN G. WHITE IN EUROPE, 1885-1887, P. 71.*

women the light of his countenance, and will give them a power that exceeds that of men. They can do in families a work that men cannot do, a work that reaches the inner life. They can come close to the hearts of those whom men cannot reach. Their labor is needed."[237] With the burden for the work, she again stated: "A direct necessity is being met by the work of women who have given themselves to the Lord and are reaching out to help a needy, sin-stricken people. Personal evangelistic work is to be done. The women who take up this work carry the gospel to the homes of the people in the highways and the byways. They read and explain the word to families, praying with them, caring for the sick, relieving their temporal necessities. They present before families and individuals the purifying, transforming influence of the truth. They show that the way to find peace and joy is to follow Jesus."[238]

Ellen White clearly did not envision women being ordained as elders or pastors. Neither did she call for or forbid it. Rather, she just plainly did not address it directly as an issue. Instead, she envisioned a large cadre of Adventist women, filled with the Spirit of God, vigorously participating in an array of personal ministries to hasten the coming of the Lord. The lack of encouragement by the church has contributed to the great vacuum created by the paid ministry. The outcry being heard today and the appropriate response will fill a void that the work of the Lord desperately needs.

Would our adoption of Ellen White's view of the role of women in the church make a difference? Absolutely! Let me review the reasons:

There would be a burgeoning increase in personal work by both paid full - and part-time workers.

It would open more opportunities for ministry on the part of women in either part-time or full-time labor, as well as volunteer workers. There would be a significant upsurge in the numbers of

---

*237 ELLEN G.WHITE, IN REVIEW AND HERALD, AUG. 26, 1902.*

*238 ELLEN G.WHITE, TESTIMONIES FOR THE CHURCH, VOL. 6, P. 118.*

people won to Christ and His truth through the ministry of women.

As godly women workers challenge men to reflect the self-sacrificing headship of Christ in their own relationship with their wives, there would be healing in the home relationships. Women would honor God's ordained headship as they would the headship of Christ.

The practice of the Lordship of Christ would make such a difference in strengthening the families. And by it, God's church would make itself available for the outpouring of the Holy Spirit through whom a hurting world filled with broken families would find healing and hope.

There would be no need to restructure the church or its polity, yet the paradigm change would revolutionize the church.
It would hasten the coming of our Lord and Savior, and we could all go home.

## OTHER POINTS IN THE CONTROVERSY

There are additional points of controversy regarding the issue of women pastors. I will list each and then address them:

*1. The Israelites were determined to have their own way and demanded to have a king. Even though God was not in favor of it, He permitted it. Therefore, though God did not condone it, He did not condemn it. An appeal for variance based on the supposition that God tolerates what He does not approve is dangerous. The books of history in the Bible are replete with the abuses, apostasies, and final overthrow of Israel resulting from getting its way in demanding a king.*

*The situation is found in 1 Samuel 8:4-10. It says:"Then all the elders of Israel gathered themselves together, and came to Samuel unto Ramah, And said unto him, Behold, thou art old, and thy sons walk not in thy ways: now make us a king to judge us like all the nations. But the thing displeased Samuel, when they said, Give us a king to judge us. And Samuel prayed unto the Lord. And the Lord said unto Samuel, Hearken unto the voice of the people in all that they say unto thee: for they have not rejected thee, but they have rejected me, that I should not reign over them. According to all the works which they have done since the day that I brought them up out of Egypt even unto this day, wherewith they have forsaken me, and served other gods, so do they also unto thee. Now therefore hearken unto their voice: howbeit yet protest solemnly unto them, and shew them the manner of the king that shall reign over them. And Samuel told all the words of the Lord unto the people that asked of him a king."*

ANSWER: The fact is that God had made provisions for a king, but with conditions. We find this in Deuteronomy 17:14-20. It says: "When thou art come unto the land which the Lord thy God giveth thee, and shalt possess it, and shalt dwell therein, and shalt say, I will set a king over me, like as all the nations that are about me; Thou shalt in any wise set him king over thee, whom the Lord thy God shall choose: one from among thy brethren shalt thou set king over thee: thou mayest not set a stranger over thee, which is not thy brother. But he shall not multiply horses to himself, nor cause the people to return to Egypt, to the end that he should multiply horses: forasmuch as the Lord hath said unto you, Ye shall henceforth return no more that way. Neither shall he multiply wives to himself, that his heart turn not away: neither shall he greatly multiply to himself silver and gold. And it shall be, when he sitteth upon the throne of his kingdom, that he shall write him a copy of this law in a book out of that which is before the priests the Levites: And it shall be with him, and he shall read therein all the days of his life: that he may learn to fear the Lord his God, to keep all the words of this law and these statutes, to do them: That his heart be not lifted up above his brethren, and that he turn not aside from the commandment, to the right hand, or to the left: to the end that he may prolong his days in his kingdom, he, and his children, in the midst of Israel."

The main issue with this is the motive. They no longer wanted God to be their leader. He was invisible. Eli and his wanton sons had been the precursors of the spiritual declension of Israel. The nation was waning spiritually as Samuel was getting older. In their spiritual stupor they had become envious of the surrounding nations and preferred to emulate the pomposity of the rival nations with kings. They preferred a visible leader. They did not consult with God, nor ask His counsel. They made their determination and gave their ultimatum to

Samuel. That is why God said, "They have not rejected thee, but they have rejected me" (1 Samuel 8:7).

To use this argument as a compromise to ordain women as pastors suggests that the same conditions prevail in the modern church that prevailed for our ancient counterpart. At least the Jews had an established precedent provided by God in His Word. There is no mandate or provision anywhere in the Bible to allow for women pastors.

*2. Deborah was the leader of Israel because she was the judge in those days. The text says: "And Deborah, a prophetess, the wife of Lapidoth, she judged Israel at that time. And she dwelt under the palm tree of Deborah between Ramah and Bethel in mount Ephraim: and the children of Israel came up to her for judgment" (Judges 4:4, 5).*

ANSWER: Deborah was not the main judge. It was Barak. That is why, as a prophet, she addressed him as the leader. The Scripture says: "And she sent and called Barak the son of Abinoam out of Kedeshnaphtali, and said unto him, Hath not the Lord God of Israel commanded, saying, Go and draw toward mount Tabor, and take with thee ten thousand men of the children of Naphtali and of the children of Zebulun? And I will draw unto thee to the river Kishon Sisera, the captain of Jabin's army, with his chariots and his multitude; and I will deliver him into thine hand" (verses 6, 7). Deborah's authority was "perhaps not as a princess by any civil authority conferred upon her, but as a prophetess, correcting abuses and redressing grievances."[239] As mentioned before, she claims the title "a mother in Israel" (Judges 5:7).

Using this example as a basis for ordaining women as pastors lacks substance. A contemporary counterpart to Deborah was Ellen White, who, while being a prophet, never took control of the reins of the church. Like Deborah, she recognized the church leaders' authority and gave them counsel. But, as stated before in this book, she was never ordained nor became the official recognized leader of the church.

---

239 *THE SDA BIBLE COMMENTARY, VOL. 2, P. 330.*

Jesus said to the religious leaders and teachers of the law in His day, "Ye do err, not knowing the scriptures, nor the power of God" (Matthew 22:29). "The Sadducees are said to have prided themselves on being more exact students of the Scriptures than the Pharisees, but Jesus here asserts that in spite of all their vaunted knowledge of the Word of God, they are profoundly ignorant. Theological concepts based on speculative reasoning from incomplete information are certain to lead astray those who resort to this fanciful method of arriving at truth. Christians today should beware lest they, too, 'err, not knowing the scriptures.'"[240]

*3. Paul was biased against women and, therefore, some of his writings cannot be inspired.*

ANSWER: Relationships from a Theological Point of View. In a review by Michelle Myers, Southwestern Baptist Theological Seminary, she writes, "Ultimately, Jewett is rejecting the inerrancy of Scripture. He is belittling God and His Word by making himself the judge and the authority over which parts of the text he chooses to believe and which he chooses not to believe."

As I have surveyed all that I could find in the Bible and the other inspired counsels and have reviewed the points of support in favor of ordaining women into the gospel ministry, I have discovered that this is not solely an issue of women's ordination. If it were, then we could all go home and rest. No, the issues are much deeper, but they are glossed over by the barrage of strategies to make the Bible say what it does not.

Paul Jewett asserted that the apostle Paul was a chauvinist and, therefore, some of his writings are not inspired. Those who support women's ordination are making similar assertions concerning biblical authors in contradiction to a plain biblical principal - holy men wrote as they were moved by the Holy Spirit, making all Scripture inspired (see 2 Timothy 3:14-17; 2 Peter 1:20, 21). This is more than an exercise in higher criticism; it is a direct undermining of the author's

---

*240 THE SDA BIBLE COMMENTARY, VOL. 2, P. 483.*

credibility and the inspiration of the Scriptures - a very dangerous position.

4. *Plea for exemption or variance based on regional circumstances.*

ANSWER: In biblical or theological matters the church has authority. "The Seventh-day Adventist form of governance is representative, which recognizes that authority rests in the membership and is expressed through duly elected representatives at each level of organization."[241] Other Christian denominations operate either under a congregationalist, papal, episcopal, or presbyterian system. All of these rest the final ecclesiastical authority in bishops, local elders, popes, or individual congregations. Each sovereign nation has its own laws. Therefore, the Adventist church allows for variances when it comes to civil laws (e.g. work laws, ordinances, or statutes). But when it comes to theology, the church - not one of its organizations or an individual -has the final say.

We are warned: "Satan hopes to involve the remnant people of God in the general ruin that is coming upon the earth. As the coming of Christ draws nigh, he will be more determined and decisive in his efforts to overthrow them. Men and women will arise professing to have some new light or some new revelation whose tendency is to unsettle faith in the old landmarks. Their doctrines will not bear the test of God's word, yet souls will be deceived."[242] "When the power of God testifies as to what is truth, that truth is to stand forever as the truth. No aftersuppositions, contrary to the light God has given are to be entertained. Men will arise with interpretations of Scripture which are to them truth, but which are not truth.

The truth for this time, God has given us as a foundation for our faith. He Himself has taught us what is truth. One will arise, and still another, with new light which contradicts the light that God has

---

*241 HTTP://ARTICLES.LATIMES.COM/1991-09-16/NEWS/MN-1627_1_SCHOLAR-AT-FULLER-FULLER-THEOLOGICAL-SEMINARY. ACCESSED JULY 1, 2014.*

*242 HTTP://BIBLICALWOMAN.COM/WP-CONTENT/UPLOADS/MYERS-REIVEW-OF-MAN-AS-MALE-AND-FEMALE.PDF*

given under the demonstration of His Holy Spirit."[243] "If there were no church discipline and government, the church would go to fragments; it could not hold together as a body."[244] Hence the admonition: "We have nothing to fear for the future, except as we shall forget the way the Lord has led us, and His teaching in our past history."[245]

"Though we have an individual work and an individual responsibility before God, we are not to follow our own independent judgment, regardless of the opinions and feelings of our brethren; for this course would lead to disorder in the church. It is the duty of ministers to respect the judgment of their brethren; but their relations to one another, as well as the doctrines they teach, should be brought to the test of the law and the testimony; then, if hearts are teachable, there will be no divisions among us."[246]

If in order to accomplish the desired goal, there is a dismissal of church authority, as has been the case with women being ordained, then the object has become greater then the entity. This position would be understandable and acceptable if we were dealing with the apostate church of Revelation 13 with all of its abuses, but rather, we are dealing with the church of God. Even the great apostles Paul and Barnabas dared not sidestep the recognized authority of the church and its leadership in Jerusalem. In its Fall Council meeting of 2013 the General Conference stated: "Decisions to pursue a course of action not in harmony with the 1990 and 1995 General Conference Session decisions (with respect to ministerial ordination) represent not only an expression of dissent but also a demonstration of self-determination in a matter previously decided by the collective Church,"[247]

---

243 *CLARK H. PINNOCK, "WHO WE ARE: OUR DIGNITY AS HUMAN: A NEO-EVANGELICAL THEOLOGY." THEOLOGY TODAY, OCT. 1997. HTTP://EN.WIKIPEDIA.ORG/WIKI/PAUL_KING_JEWETT. ACCESSED JULY 1, 2014.*

244 *ELLEN G. WHITE, TESTIMONIES FOR THE CHURCH, VOL. 3, P. 428.*

245 *ELLEN G. WHITE, CHRISTIAN EXPERIENCE AND TEACHINGS OF ELLEN G. WHITE, P. 204.*

246 *IBID., P. 203.*

247 HTTP://NEWS.ADVENTIST.ORG/ALL-NEWS/NEWS/GO/2012-10-16/AFTER-DEBATE-ANNUAL-COUNCIL-VOTES-STATEMENT-ON-CHURCH-POLITY. *ACCESSED SEPTEMBER 10, 2014.*

We have been counseled: "It is necessary that our unity today be of a character that will bear the test of trial. . . . We have many lessons to learn, and many, many to unlearn. God and heaven alone are infallible. Those who think that they will never have to give up a cherished view, never have occasion to change an opinion, will be disappointed. As long as we hold to our own ideas and opinions with determined persistency, we cannot have the unity for which Christ prayed. When a brother receives new light upon the Scriptures, he should frankly explain his position, and every minister should search the Scriptures with the spirit of candor to see if the points presented can be substantiated by the Inspired Word. "The servant of the Lord must not strive; but be gentle unto all men, apt to teach, patient, in meekness instructing those that oppose themselves; if God peradventure will give them repentance to the acknowledging of the truth." 2 Timothy 2:24, 25."[248]

---

*248 ELLEN G. WHITE, TESTIMONIES TO MINISTERS AND GOSPEL WORKERS, PP. 30, 31.*

For additional copies of this book,
please contact the author at:

louisrtorres@gmail.com

NOTES:

NOTES:

NOTES:

NOTES:

NOTES:

NOTES: